Off the

a farce

Derek Benfield

SAMUELFRENCH.COM

SAMUELFRENCH-LONDON.CO.UK

FOR AMATEUR PRODUCTION ENQUIRIES

UNITED KINGDOM AND WORLD
EXCLUDING NORTH AMERICA
plays@SamuelFrench-London.co.uk
020 7255 4302/01

Each title is subject to availability from Samuel French,

depending upon country of performance.

OFF THE HOOK!

LIST OF CHARACTERS

NORAH CATCHPOLE

EDNA, her sister

FRED BAXTER

MAJOR CATCHPOLE

CHARLIE MULLINS

HAROLD SPOOK

MRS. FLETCHER-BREWER

CAROL, her daughter

POLLY

MR. PARKINSON

The action takes place in the lounge bar of Hook House, a quiet English hotel somewhere in the country. The time is the present.

ACT I   An afternoon in Spring

ACT II   The same evening

ACT III   The early hours of the next morning

No character in this play is intended to resemble any specific person, living or dead.

OFF THE HOOK!

ACT ONE

The lounge bar of Hook House Hotel. It is oak timbered and attractive, with a log fire in the grate D.L., above which is a door leading to the dining-room. There is a small bar in the corner U.L., from which an arch leads to the kitchen and other bars, and behind which is a window. The front door is U.C. The staircase is U.R., broken by a landing, which leads off through an arch to the bedrooms. There is a cupboard door beneath the stairs and another door D.R. to the television room. A comfortable sofa is D.R.C. with a coffee table below it. Various other armchairs with loose covers where possible, one near the fireplace. Throughout the play L. and R. refer to the actors' L. and R.

It is a sunny Spring afternoon. As the curtain rises, NORAH CATCHPOLE is coming briskly down the stairs. She is a plump 45, loud-voiced and of a cheerful disposition.

NORAH   Catchpole!   (She crosses to the bar and calls again.)
                   Catchpole!

                   (EDNA, her sister, comes in from D.R. She is the
                   opposite of NORAH in temperament, being somewhat
                   gloomy and serious. She is armed with a dustpan and
                   brush. NORAH sees her and they meet C.)

	Didn't you 'ear me calling?
EDNA	I'd have had to be deaf not to.
NORAH	Then why didn't you answer?
EDNA	My name ain't Catchpole.
NORAH	I'm surprised you know what your name is. Where is he?
EDNA	Round the back chasing the pigs. They're out again.
NORAH	Those pigs are more out than in. I wish he'd get that gate mended.
EDNA	Shall I go and fetch him?
NORAH	You'd never prise him away from those pigs. Never mind. I'll 'ave to do it.
EDNA	Do what?
NORAH	Chase the milkman.
EDNA	You'll end up in the "News of the World".
NORAH	What are you talking about?
EDNA	You! Running after the milkman!
NORAH	Don't be daft! We 'aven't paid him for three weeks.

(NORAH goes off through the door D.L. The minute she has gone, the front door bursts open and FRED BAXTER comes in. He is a heavily built Cockney of about 48, wearing a Harris tweed suit, a pork pie hat and carrying a suitcase. He comes straight down to EDNA.)

FRED	I'm looking for the guv'nor.
EDNA	Well, it ain't me. (She kneels down abruptly with her dustpan and brush.)
FRED	Where is he?
EDNA	Out the back chasing the pigs.
FRED	And his wife?
EDNA	Out the front chasing the milkman.
FRED	Then you'll 'ave to do it. (He pulls her to her feet.)

EDNA	Do what?
FRED	The booking.
EDNA	Cleaning is what I do. Bookings is out of my province.
FRED	Well, when the guv'nor's chasing pigs and his wife's chasing the tradesmen, <u>who</u> does do the booking?
EDNA	They've never been caught chasing before. Not both at the same time.
FRED	Come on, then! (He leads her to the bar where the register is kept.)
EDNA	(alarmed) What you doing?
FRED	There's a first time for everything. It can't be all that difficult. (As she looks blank.) Just give me a number!
EDNA	(brightening) Oh, I know <u>that</u> game!
FRED	It isn't a game! Give me the number of a room.
EDNA	I don't think we've got one.
FRED	Then where would you like me to sleep?
EDNA	Don't you get saucy with me.
FRED	(patiently) I just want a room.
EDNA	All the rooms is occupied.
FRED	All of them?
EDNA	Yes. I take it that isn't the style of room you 'ad in mind?
FRED	(loudly) No, of course it isn't!
EDNA	Don't you shout at me. I'm not 'ere for shouting at. Cleaning is what I'm 'ere for.
FRED	Yes, I know that!
EDNA	Cleaning's one thing and shouting's another. I can do cleaning, I won't 'ave shouting and I can't do booking.
FRED	(exasperated) Then find me somebody who can!

(MAJOR CATCHPOLE comes in D.L. He is in his mid-fifties, balding and moustached with a military bearing. His speech is rather mannered, and the refined overtones he endeavours to assume do not always conceal the Cockney lurking beneath the surface.)

CATCHPOLE   Those bloody pigs'll be the end of me!   (He sees FRED.)   Oh, I beg your pardon.

EDNA   (nudging FRED)   There he is!

FRED   What?

EDNA   That's 'im!

FRED   Who?

EDNA   Go on - grab 'im!   (She takes hold of FRED and pushes him towards CATCHPOLE.)

CATCHPOLE   (horrified)   Edna! What you think you're doing?

EDNA   I'm getting on with the cleaning, Mr. Catchpole.

CATCHPOLE   Yes. I think you'd better.

(EDNA goes out into the dining-room. CATCHPOLE turns apologetically to FRED.)

My sister-in-law. Rather 'orrible, I'm afraid.

FRED   But she called you "Mr. Catchpole".

CATCHPOLE   Ah, yes. Sign of respect. Only thing in her favour. Never remembers my rank, though.

FRED   Rank?

CATCHPOLE   (coming smartly to attention)   Major Catchpole at your service!

FRED   Aah!

CATCHPOLE   What?

FRED   So you're it? You're the guv'nor?

CATCHPOLE   The proprietor - yes.

FRED   Good. I want a room.

CATCHPOLE   We haven't got one.

FRED	Now don't you start! As a matter of fact I want three rooms.
CATCHPOLE	(eyeing him suspiciously) Only a very furtive sort of man would want three rooms.
FRED	I have two friends!
CATCHPOLE	Close friends?
FRED	Not very. That's why I want three rooms.
CATCHPOLE	You're out of luck, sir. All our rooms is heavily booked. Except for the box room, and that's over the kitchen with a terrible smell of cookin'. I couldn't recommend that. Be a bit of a tight squeeze for three.
FRED	Look - I 'ave arranged to stay 'ere!
CATCHPOLE	I'd like to help you, sir, but the only three rooms we have left has been booked by a Mr. Baxter.
FRED	That's me! I'm Baxter!
CATCHPOLE	Then why the 'ell didn't you say so?
	(He crosses to the register with FRED following him.)
	Here we are - Baxter, Baxter and Baxter.
FRED	I said they were my friends, not my brothers.
CATCHPOLE	I see. Then what are the names of the other gentlemen? (He waits, pen at the ready.)
FRED	Mullins and Spook.
CATCHPOLE	(doubtfully) Baxter, Mullins and Spook?
FRED	That's right.
CATCHPOLE	Sounds like the music hall.
FRED	I don't care what it sounds like!
CATCHPOLE	Great pity that.
FRED	Eh?
CATCHPOLE	The dyin' of the music 'all. Great loss.
FRED	(trying to be patient) Will you please give me the

	number of my room?
CATCHPOLE	Ah - no numbers.
FRED	What d'you mean?
CATCHPOLE	You're in "Oak", sir.
FRED	Oak?
CATCHPOLE	(with a benign smile) All the rooms is named after trees. Quite a novel idea, I thought. You'll be in "Oak", Mr. Mullins in "Ash" and Mr. Spook in "Willow".
FRED	(unimpressed) How the 'ell do we know where they are?
CATCHPOLE	You'll soon get used to it.
	(NORAH, a trifle breathless, comes in from the front door.)
	Ah, Norah! You're just in time to take Mr. Baxter to his bedroom.
NORAH	(coming down to R. of FRED) A pleasure, I'm sure.
CATCHPOLE	This here is my wife.
FRED	(to NORAH) Did you get him?
NORAH	Eh?
FRED	(playfully) Did you catch the milkman?
NORAH	No. He saw me coming and went off down the path like greased lightning.
CATCHPOLE	(quietly) Can't say I blame him.
NORAH	What did you say?
CATCHPOLE	Nothing, dear. Mr. Baxter will be staying here for a few days with two of his friends.
NORAH	(to FRED) Why? Couldn't you find anywhere better?
CATCHPOLE	My wife - she's a bit of a comic. I can assure you we'll do everything we can to make your stay a pleasant one. (He goes to put the register away.)

NORAH	Yes, of course we will.
	(Unseen by CATCHPOLE, NORAH gives FRED a quick pinch on the bottom and crosses to get his case from near the stairs. FRED reacts.)
CATCHPOLE	Perhaps you'd show Mr. Baxter to his room, Norah. He'll be sleeping in "Oak".
NORAH	Very nice, too. Come on, Mr. Baxter. After you. (She stands back to let him go first.)
FRED	(guardedly) Er - no - please - you go first.
	(She goes off upstairs. FRED starts to follow.)
CATCHPOLE	She's a good woman at bottom.
FRED	Yes, I'm sure she is.
CATCHPOLE	Means well, you know. But, of course, she's not exactly one of the 'ierarchy.
FRED	'ierarchy?
CATCHPOLE	Not exactly the upper crust.
FRED	Oh.
CATCHPOLE	I married a trifle beneath me, you see. When I married 'er, it was like a King marryin' a commoner.
FRED	Yes - and they don't come much commoner than 'er! (He rubs his behind.)
	(NORAH re-appears at the top of the stairs.)
NORAH	Come on, Mr. Baxter! Don't you loiter on the landing!
FRED	Just coming. (With a doubtful look, he goes off up the stairs. As he does so, EDNA races on from the dining-room and goes quickly to CATCHPOLE.)
EDNA	Mr. Catchpole! Mr. Catchpole! There's a car! It's stopping outside!
CATCHPOLE	What do you expect it to do? Drive straight into the lounge?
EDNA	I thought you'd like to know.

CATCHPOLE	Well, now I <u>do</u> know, so I'm a wiser and 'appier man, ain't I?
	(The front door opens and CHARLIE MULLINS comes in. He is about 37, a pleasant young man wearing a light suit and a gay tie.)
CHARLIE	I say! Did you know there are three pigs running about in the car park?
CATCHPOLE	Oh, blast 'em! They've got out again! (He pushes the astonished CHARLIE aside and races out of the front door, closing it behind him.)
CHARLIE	Are you his wife?
EDNA	No fear. She's elsewhere.
CHARLIE	Does he always rush about after the pigs like that?
EDNA	The pigs' place is out the back.
CHARLIE	I should jolly well hope so.
EDNA	The car park is for <u>cars</u>. The <u>sty</u> is for pigs.
CHARLIE	What an excellent arrangement!
EDNA	Not for the pigs.
CHARLIE	They prefer the car park?
EDNA	Or the dining-room.
CHARLIE	You have pigs in the dining-room? I mean, apart from the residents?
EDNA	We did last week. Right in the middle of lunch. Ran round the room twice and out the back door.
CHARLIE	Did anybody complain?
EDNA	Nobody seemed to notice.
CHARLIE	They must have been in the middle of soup.
EDNA	Was you expected?
CHARLIE	Yes, I was. I mean, I am. An hour ago. Have you got a Mr. Baxter?
EDNA	He's upstairs with Mrs. Catchpole.

CHARLIE	At this time of day? Good heavens! Who's she?
EDNA	(gesturing after CATCHPOLE) She's 'is wife – my sister.
CHARLIE	I thought you said she was elsewhere?
EDNA	She's elsewhere upstairs.
CHARLIE	With Mr. Baxter.
EDNA	Showing him his room.
CHARLIE	Hasn't he seen it before?
EDNA	Not with 'er inside.
CHARLIE	Well, perhaps you'd better show me mine.
EDNA	Don't you start!
CHARLIE	I beg your pardon?
EDNA	I 'ad enough of that with the last one. And when I wouldn't do it, he shouted at me.
CHARLIE	Good heavens! What did he want you to do?
EDNA	The bookings.
CHARLIE	Oh, is that all?
	(There is a knocking at the front door.)
EDNA	And there's another one! (Calling.) All right! All right! I'm coming! (She goes and opens the front door.)
	(HAROLD SPOOK is there. He is a quiet, brow-beaten little North Countryman of about 40. He is wearing an ill-fitting blue suit. His ankles are tied together with cord and his hands tied behind his back.)
CHARLIE	Don't stand on ceremony, Spook. Come on in.
	(HAROLD hops into the centre of the room. CHARLIE and EDNA come to either side of him.)
	You took a long time getting out of the car.
HAROLD	What do you expect – trussed up like this?

CHARLIE	That's all right. You'll be ready for Christmas.
EDNA	(gazing at him in wonder) What you all tied up for?
CHARLIE	He's a very nervous traveller. Will keep jumping about. I <u>had</u> to tie him up.
HAROLD	Did you have to put me in the boot, as well?
CHARLIE	I didn't want people to see you. Not the state you were in.
HAROLD	Oh, it <u>was</u> uncomfortable in there. I bet I've got the pattern of that spare wheel all over my arse.
CHARLIE	We don't want to hear about that, thank you very much! Where are your manners? Just look at this lady. She's gone pale at the mere mention. (To EDNA.) Haven't you? (To HAROLD.) Yes. Pale as chalk.
HAROLD	(miserably) I didn't want to come 'ere in the first place.
CHARLIE	It's a damn sight better than the place you <u>were</u> in.
HAROLD	Well, <u>I</u> don't like the look of it much.
CHARLIE	How can you be so ungrateful? What will this lady think of you? She works away, cleaning and scrubbing, to make the place pleasant and comfortable for you – (To EDNA.) You do do that, don't you?
EDNA	Yes, I do do that.
CHARLIE	There you are. She do do that. And what thanks does she get? A happy smile and a thank-you-very-much? Oh, dear me, no! Coarse language and a face like a fish.
EDNA	(to HAROLD) Wouldn't you like to sit down, Mr. – er – ?
CHARLIE	Spook.
HAROLD	Eh? That's not my –
CHARLIE	(quickly) Harold Spook.
EDNA	He ought to sit down, oughtn't he?

CHARLIE   After what he said about his anatomy I doubt if he could.

EDNA   (to HAROLD)   Come on, dear. I'll give you a hand.

             (With EDNA's assistance, HAROLD hops to the sofa and
             sits down. He first utters a cry of pain, then a sigh of
             relief as he settles down.)

HAROLD   Thanks very much.

EDNA   'Ere - I'll untie you.   (She starts to do so.)

CHARLIE   And don't you start waving your arms about again. We
             don't want you causing any carnage.

HAROLD   I wish you'd left me where I was.

CHARLIE   Don't you speak like that, Spook! To think what I've
             done for you - risked life and limb - and that's all the
             thanks I get.

             (EDNA has now freed HAROLD from his bonds. He
             wiggles his ankles.)

HAROLD   (pleased)   Hey - look!

CHARLIE   What?

HAROLD   They're moving!

CHARLIE   What do you expect them to do?

             (CATCHPOLE races in, breathless, from the front door.)

CATCHPOLE   Edna - quick! Come and give me a hand! I can't deal
             with the old sow single-'anded!

             (He races out again, followed by an obedient EDNA.)

HAROLD   What was all that?

CHARLIE   You'll get used to it. You might have given the game
             away - hopping in here tied up like a parcel.

HAROLD   I couldn't stay out there all night.

CHARLIE   I'd have come and got you. And as for all that talk
             about wishing you'd been left where you were - !

HAROLD   Well, so I do.

CHARLIE   Don't you realise how lucky you are? Just you think of all those other poor chaps. I bet they envy you to-night, all locked up in their cells. You're the lucky one.

HAROLD   You call that lucky? Being pushed out through the lavatory window, up over the wall and down onto the roof of a van? I didn't want all the fuss.

CHARLIE   Well, you couldn't have just walked out of the gate, could you?

HAROLD   (sulkily)   Nobody asked me if I wanted to get out.

CHARLIE   We took it for granted! I mean, it wasn't exactly the Hilton, was it? They weren't bringing in smoked trout and a glass of Chablis.

HAROLD   I was quite comfortable.

CHARLIE   In there?

HAROLD   Gave me time to think. It's so noisy at home. I never get the chance.

CHARLIE   Well, if you're so keen on it, I'm sure they'd be glad to see you back again! Might even get a cup of tea with the Governor.

HAROLD   Right. I'll go now, then –

          (He starts to rise, but CHARLIE restrains him.)

CHARLIE   Not yet. Not yet, Harold. We've got things to do here first.

HAROLD   'Ave we?

CHARLIE   We didn't get you out just for the fun of it, you know. We'll get this little business settled in no time, and then we can all go anywhere we like!

HAROLD   (puzzled)   What little business?

CHARLIE   (moving towards the front door)   Where the hell's that proprietor? He must have put his pigs away by now. (He opens the door and goes out, calling.)   I say, are you there?

          (NORAH comes down the stairs. She sees HAROLD. It is love at first sight. She moves down to the sofa, gazing at him. He shifts uncomfortably.)

NORAH	Who are you?
HAROLD	Eh?
NORAH	Are you staying 'ere?
HAROLD	Yes.
NORAH	(with a knowing smile) You must be Ash or Willow.
HAROLD	No. Spook.
NORAH	Willow's next to my room.
HAROLD	(alarmed) Is it?
NORAH	So you'll know where I am, won't you?
HAROLD	Aye. I'll know where your 'usband is, an' all!

(She laughs and gives him a nudge. He falls off the sofa onto the floor. She goes to help him up, but he misinterprets her advance and is struggling to get away from her as CHARLIE and CATCHPOLE come in from the front door and react to the scene.)

CHARLIE   Harold!

(NORAH moves away from HAROLD and he gets up, sheepishly.)

CATHPOLE   This would be Mr. Spook, I take it?

CHARLIE   Yes. You take it right.   (To HAROLD.)   What are you doing?

HAROLD   I'm hungry.

CHARLIE   What's that got to do with it?

CATCHPOLE   Come this way, gentlemen, and I will personally escort you to your rooms. Norah, you fetch the luggage from the car.

NORAH   The car - yes, right.   (Aside to HAROLD as she passes.)   I'll see you later!

(As she goes behind CHARLIE on her way out, she gives him a smart pinch on the behind and goes out, smiling. CHARLIE reacts to the pinch.)

CHARLIE   Don't stand there gawping, Harold.

CATCHPOLE   (going up the stairs)   You'll be in Ash and Mr. Spook
                will be in Willow.

HAROLD   (fearfully)   Aye, and I know where that is!

CHARLIE   We're not in the annexe, are we?

CATCHPOLE   Oh, no, sir! All the rooms is named after trees. This
                way, sir.   (He leads the way off.)

CHARLIE   You hear that, Spook? Your room is a tree. So, for
                God's sake, don't fall out of bed or you'll break your
                bloody neck!

                (They go off up the stairs. Immediately they have
                disappeared, the front door opens and MRS. FLETCHER-
                BREWER and her daughter CAROL come in. MRS.
                FLETCHER-BREWER is tall, with greying hair and a
                severe manner. She is wearing a raincoat over a tweed
                suit, Wellington boots and a trilby hat. She is carrying
                fishing tackle which she puts down inside the doorway.
                CAROL is about 25, very pretty and wearing boots and a
                raincoat under which is a skirt and sweater. During the
                opening dialogue they remove their coats and hang them
                up near the front door.)

MRS. F-B   I shall speak to the proprietor! If it isn't bad enough to
                go fishing in a stream with no fish, I come back to find
                another car lodged in my bay. And a red sports car into
                the bargain! It doesn't augur well, Carol. It doesn't
                augur well at all.

CAROL   Mummy, there was plenty of room elsewhere.

MRS. F-B   I have been parking in that particular bay for seven days
                now. Elsewhere is for other people.

                (The front door opens and NORAH comes in, carrying a
                suitcase and a leather grip. She pauses on her way to the
                stairs.)

NORAH   'Ave any luck, dear?

MRS. F-B   (with a withering look)   When I go fishing, Mrs.
                Catchpole, luck has little to do with it.

NORAH	Oh? You did well, then?
MRS. F-B	No. That stream is devoid of fish.
NORAH	Oh, there were a lot there the other day. Lovely big fellows! Saw them meself. Perhaps you're using the wrong bait. (She makes for the stairs.)
MRS. F-B	Mrs. Catchpole!
NORAH	Yes, dear?
MRS. F-B	Who is the owner of that – (Pause.) – red car?
NORAH	Oh, that belongs to Mr. Mullins. Lovely, isn't it? Bet you'd like to have a spin in that, eh? (She goes off upstairs.)
MRS. F-B	(thoughtfully) Mr. Mullins. Well, I shall be ready for him. Now, Carol, perhaps you'd be good enough to order tea.
CAROL	All right, Mummy.
MRS. F-B	I'm going to change out of these boots. (She starts to go up the stairs.) And if Major Catchpole should appear, say that I am looking for him! (She sweeps off through the arch.)
	(CAROL is about to cross towards the door D.L. when it opens abruptly and EDNA is there.)
EDNA	Oh – you're back, then. That means you'll be wanting something.
CAROL	Er – yes, please, Edna.
EDNA	(as one sentence) Will you 'ave tea or drinks it's a bit late for tea will you 'ave drinks?
CAROL	I think my mother would prefer tea.
EDNA	Yes. I thought she would. Well, I can't do it.
CAROL	Why not?
EDNA	Because it's not my job. Cleaning and general is what I do.
CAROL	Oh. (She sits on the sofa.) Well, if you asked

	the cook awfully nicely perhaps she'd do it?
EDNA	I doubt it.
CAROL	(patiently) Well, will you please go and try?
EDNA	(going) If you like. (She turns at the door.) Won't do no good.
CAROL	Why not?
EDNA	It's the cook's afternoon off. (She goes out D.L.)

(The moment she has gone, CHARLIE comes down the stairs.)

CHARLIE	What an absolutely rotten hotel this is! (He stops as he sets eyes on CAROL, and smiles.) At least, I thought it was.
CAROL	Good afternoon.
CHARLIE	Yes, isn't it? You weren't here just now.
CAROL	Wasn't I?
CHARLIE	I'm sure I'd have noticed you.
CAROL	Would you?
CHARLIE	Oh, yes! I remember looking around. There was nothing at all like you.
CAROL	I just came in. I've been fishing.
CHARLIE	So you have! You've still got your – er – (He points at her boots.)
CAROL	Boots on.
CHARLIE	Yes, of course – that's what they're called! You've got them on very well, too. I've never met anyone who had boots on as well as all that.
CAROL	I ought to go and change.
CHARLIE	(eagerly) Shall I give you a hand? With your boots.
CAROL	I don't think I know your name.
CHARLIE	It's Charlie Mullins.

CAROL	(alarmed) Mullins?
CHARLIE	Don't you like it? If you don't like it, I'll change it.
CAROL	Oh, I like it all right. I was just wondering how it would appeal to my mother.
	(CHARLIE looks puzzled.)
	How do you do, Mr. Mullins. (She holds out her hand.)
CHARLIE	Oh, yes. (He sits beside her and takes her extended hand.) How do you do. (He gazes at her admiringly.)
CAROL	(with a little smile) I'm Carol Fletcher-Brewer.
CHARLIE	(gazing at her) Of course you are!
CAROL	Can I have it back, please?
CHARLIE	H'm?
CAROL	My hand.
CHARLIE	Oh, is this yours? So it is. (He releases her hand reluctantly.) Are you staying here?
CAROL	For a few days.
CHARLIE	What a lovely hotel this is!
	(MRS. FLETCHER-BREWER comes sailing downstairs, having changed out of her boots. She is followed by MAJOR CATCHPOLE at his most obsequious.)
MRS. F-B	(as she enters) I don't care how you do it, Major Catchpole, provided it is done.
CATCHPOLE	I will personally expedite matters.
MRS. F-B	I hope so.
	(She sees CAROL and CHARLIE, and CHARLIE rises hurriedly.)
	No sign of that tea?
CAROL	There seems to be a bit of a hitch.
MRS. F-B	Hitch?

CAROL	In the kitchen.
MRS. F-B	A hitch in the kitchen? (She turns to CATCHPOLE.) Do you hear that, Major? All is not smooth running in your kitchen.
CATCHPOLE	Ah, no, madam - the cook isn't there.
MRS. F-B	(imperiously) Not there? Then where?
CATCHPOLE	It's her afternoon off, madam. She's up in town visiting her mother. Terrible legs she's got.
CHARLIE	I don't think we want to hear about the cook's legs, do we?
CATCHPOLE	Not the cook's - her mother's.
CHARLIE	Well, if they're anything like the cook's they'll be terrible!
	(His smile dies as MRS. FLETCHER-BREWER glares at him.)
CATCHPOLE	I'll go and see to the tea myself, madam.
MRS. F-B	You? Cutting bread-and-butter? A man in your position?
CHARLIE	(to CATCHPOLE) What position do you cut bread-and-butter in?
MRS. F-B	Surely your wife could manage that small function?
CATCHPOLE	She's upstairs - seeing to the gentlemen.
MRS. F-B	She seems to spend her life lingering in bedrooms. You'll have to speak to her about it. I also noticed her earlier this afternoon - running after the milkman, shouting loudly.
CATCHPOLE	Yes, but he was too fast for her!
	(EDNA bursts in D.L. with a tray of tea for two and slams it down on the bar.)
EDNA	There you are! Only remember - I'm not supposed to carry trays.
CHARLIE	Why? What have you done to yourself?
EDNA	It's out of my province. That's right, isn't it, Mr. Catchpole?

CATCHPOLE	I thought perhaps on the cook's afternoon off you could stretch a point.
EDNA	(reluctantly) All right – but this is as far as I go. I'll carry it in, but I'm not serving! (She goes out D.L.)
MRS. F–B	Well, really!
CATCHPOLE	(obsequiously) Tea is served, madam.
MRS. F–B	I could hardly have been unaware of that! We'll have it over here.
	(She sits beside CAROL on the sofa. CATCHPOLE makes for the tray, but CHARLIE gets there first.)
CHARLIE	Allow me! We can't have you carrying trays. Not a man in your position.
CATCHPOLE	Ah, you will have your little joke, sir. (He goes out D.L.)
	(CHARLIE carries the tray across to the ladies and puts it down on the coffee table in front of them.)
CHARLIE	Your tea, madam.
MRS. F–B	Thank you. I'm relieved to see that at least somebody here is civilised.
CHARLIE	Oh, yes. I'm very that.
MRS. F–B	Have you just started working here, young man?
CAROL	Mummy, he's staying here!
MRS. F–B	Oh, I do beg your pardon! In that case perhaps you'd join us in our tea?
CHARLIE	Is there room for us all?
CAROL	I'll ring for another cup. (She starts to rise.)
	(EDNA comes in with an extra cup and saucer.)
EDNA	Did you want another cup?
CHARLIE	(turning to MRS. FLETCHER–BREWER with a smile) The service here is remarkable.

CAROL   (resuming her seat)   I was just going to ring.

EDNA   Then I've saved you the trouble, 'aven't I?

CAROL   Yes. Thank you.

CHARLIE   (taking the cup and saucer)   You must have been psychic.

EDNA   Well, whatever I am it's only on the cook's day off! (She goes out D.L.)

             (MRS. FLETCHER-BREWER sees to the tea. CHARLIE brings up a chair and sits down near to CAROL, gazing at her.)

MRS. F-B   (busy with the tea)   How do you like it?

CHARLIE   (his eyes on CAROL)   Oh, very nice indeed!

MRS. F-B   With or without milk and sugar?

CHARLIE   (still entranced)   Yes.

MRS. F-B   Which?

CHARLIE   (coming to)   Ah! - yes - with milk and without sugar.

             (As she starts to pour.)

             No - the other way round.

MRS. F-B   I can't pour it the other way round!

CHARLIE   I mean with sugar and without milk.

             (MRS. FLETCHER-BREWER pours his tea and passes it to him via CAROL.)

             Thank you.

MRS. F-B   (as she pours some for herself and CAROL)   Perhaps you'd better help yourself to sugar.

CHARLIE   What a good idea!

             (Optional business: CHARLIE tries to get a lump of sugar onto a spoon, but only succeeds in shooting it up into the air, never to be seen again. MRS. FLETCHER-BREWER glares at him. CAROL giggles. CHARLIE grins and tries again, sends up another lump into the air and catches it neatly in his cup as it comes down. He stirs his tea happily.)

MRS. F-B   Will you be staying here very long?

CHARLIE   A few days. I gather your daughter is, too.   (He smiles at CAROL.)

CAROL   Yes, I am.

CHARLIE   (enthusiastically)   Good!

MRS. F-B   And so am I.

CHARLIE   Not so good.

CAROL   Are you here for the fishing?

CHARLIE   Oh, no. Just on holiday.

MRS. F-B   You'll find it very peaceful here. I come here occasionally to get away from the rigours of Court.

CHARLIE   Court?   (He sips his tea.)

MRS. F-B   Yes. I'm a Justice of the Peace.

     (CHARLIE almost chokes on his tea. MRS. FLETCHER-BREWER glares at him. CAROL pats him on the back helpfully.)

     What on earth is the matter?

CHARLIE   I don't think that sugar had melted properly.

MRS. F-B   It's a very interesting job being a J.P.

CHARLIE   Yes, I'm sure.

MRS. F-B   You come across some funny people on the Bench.

CHARLIE   You mean in front of it or behind it?

MRS. F-B   I was referring to the criminal classes.

CHARLIE   Oh, them? Yes, they're a horrid-looking lot, aren't they?

MRS. F-B   I pride myself in having an eye for a criminal.

CHARLIE   (alarmed)   Do you?

MRS. F-B	I can recognise one by the way he uses his hands.
CHARLIE	Really? (He hides his hands in his armpits.)
MRS. F-B	Or by the tone of his voice.
CHARLIE	You can? (He coughs and changes pitch.) You can? (He starts to choke again and quickly lifts his cup and takes a sip.)
MRS. F-B	Even by the way he sips his tea. (CHARLIE splutters and quickly gets rid of his cup again.) (With a big smile.) But, of course, when I'm on holiday I don't notice any of these things.
CHARLIE	(quietly) Thank God for that! Will you have some cake?
MRS. F-B	No, thank you, Mr. - er - I don't think you ever told us your name.
CHARLIE	I told her.
MRS. F-B	You did not tell me.
CHARLIE	Didn't I? How very rude. Now, let me see, what is it? I knew it yesterday.
CAROL	Fred Smith!
CHARLIE	(looking at her in surprise) Who's he?
CAROL	Isn't that your name?
CHARLIE	No, of course it isn't. Ah, yes - now I remember! Charlie Mullins.
MRS. F-B	Charlie?
CHARLIE	Yes. Mullins.
MRS. F-B	(severely) Mullins?
CHARLIE	Yes.
MRS. F-B	Charlie Mullins?
CHARLIE	Yes. I think you've got it now.
MRS. F-B	(ominously) Red sports car!

CHARLIE	Yes – that's right! Do you like it?
MRS. F-B	I do not like where it is standing.
CHARLIE	Don't you? (To CAROL.) Where is it standing?
MRS. F-B	You have trespassed in my bay!
CHARLIE	Have I? I never knew that. (To CAROL.) I've never done that sort of thing before. (To MRS. FLETCHER-BREWER.) I'm very sorry.
CAROL	There you are, Mummy. I knew he'd apologise.
CHARLIE	(rising) I'll go and move it right away if it'll make you happy.
MRS. F-B	It certainly will.
CHARLIE	Oh, good! I don't like the look of you –
MRS. F-B	What?
CHARLIE	– when you're unhappy. (To CAROL.) I bet she frightens the life out of them on the Bench.
	(HAROLD comes downstairs, followed by NORAH.)
NORAH	But I 'aven't finished showing you your room yet.
HAROLD	I don't need a conducted tour – it's only eight foot by six!
MRS. F-B	Mrs. Catchpole! Do you think you could drag yourself away from the bedrooms for a moment to assist your husband in the kitchen? It would be a pity if dinner was late again this evening.
NORAH	Cook not back yet?
MRS. F-B	She's with her mother.
NORAH	(crossing L.) Yes – I bet! (Chuckling to herself.) With her mother indeed!
CAROL	Don't you believe her?
NORAH	Why should I? Her mother's been dead three years. (She goes out D.L.)
	(MRS. FLETCHER-BREWER turns to peer appraisingly at

HAROLD, and is not too impressed by what she sees.)

MRS. F—B   So <u>this</u> is one of your friends, eh, Mr. Mullins?

CHARLIE   Yes.

MRS. F—B   H'm.

CHARLIE   I'm afraid he's not looking his best.

HAROLD   What do you expect? Look at this suit!   (He demonstrates the loose fitting jacket.)   Was this the best you could find me?

(CHARLIE turns to the ladies, laughing weakly.)

CHARLIE   It was his birthday present from me.

HAROLD   (surprised)   Birthday?

CHARLIE   (firmly)   Yes, Harold - birthday. You must remember. I sang "Happy birthday" to you all the way down. (To the others.)   He's very forgetful.

HAROLD   Why didn't you get me the right size, then? Just look at it! It's all baggy in the bottom!   (He demonstrates.)

CHARLIE   You'll grow into it. It's not my fault if you're a funny shape.

HAROLD   I don't like the colour, either.

CHARLIE   Well, it's better than the grey one you had on this morning!

CAROL   I think it's a nice colour.

HAROLD   (coyly)   Do you? Get away! Do you really?

CHARLIE   (to CAROL)   Don't encourage him. He's bad enough already. Just look at him. Gone all pink like a sunset.

MRS. F—B   (patiently)   Are we ever to have the pleasure of an introduction?

CHARLIE   It's no pleasure, I can assure you. Come on, Harold - over here.

(HAROLD joins him.)

	This is Harold Spook.
MRS. F-B	(puzzled) Spoke?
CHARLIE	Spoke? <u>Spook</u>!
CAROL	Spoke-Spook?
CHARLIE	Not Spoke-Spook! Spook!
MRS. F-B	Spoke-Spook-Spook?
CHARLIE	Shall we start again? This is Harold Spook.
CAROL	Oh! (To MRS. FLETCHER-BREWER.) Spook.
CHARLIE	That's right! We made it at last. Harold, this is Mrs. Fletcher-Brewer and her daughter Carol.
HAROLD	(shaking CAROL's hand) Pleased to meet you, Mrs. Fletcher-Brewer.
CHARLIE	Not that one, you fool! The other one!
HAROLD	You what?
CHARLIE	The one with the hat!
HAROLD	(moving along to MRS. FLETCHER-BREWER) Pleased to meet you.
MRS. F-B	(coldly) How do you do.
HAROLD	Very well, thank you.
MRS. F-B	It's a very unusual name.
HAROLD	What name?
MRS. F-B	Spook.
HAROLD	Well, there aren't many Fletcher-Brewers where I come from!
CAROL	Are you married?
HAROLD	Yes. I've got a wife and three kids.
CHARLIE	Just think of it — a houseful of Spooks.
MRS. F-B	(fearfully) Are they staying here with you?
HAROLD	They don't even know I'm here! They think I'm still

inside.

(The ladies react. CHARLIE hastens to cover-up.)

MRS. F-B	Inside?
CHARLIE	Inside the place where they left him.
CAROL	Well, where did they leave him?
HAROLD	They were at the house when I was taken off.
MRS. F-B	Taken off where?
CHARLIE	To hospital! He was taken off to hospital.
HAROLD	Was I?
CHARLIE	Nothing serious, you know. Just a small operation.
CAROL	Oh, dear. What was the trouble?
CHARLIE	Hammer toes.
HAROLD	'Ere!
CHARLIE	You remember, Harold! They were beating away like a pair of bongo drums. Something had to be done. So they took him in and did it.
MRS. F-B	So what's he doing here?
HAROLD	That's what I'd like to –
CHARLIE	Recuperating. I thought a little fresh air would do him the world of good. Afterwards, we'll take him back to his wife as good as new.
CAROL	She will be surprised to see him.
HAROLD	Aye, she will that! As far as she's concerned, I'm still inside –
CHARLIE	Harold! (Warningly.) Mrs. Fletcher-Brewer is a Justice of the Peace.
HAROLD	A Justice of the what?
CHARLIE	Peace.
HAROLD	She's not!
CHARLIE	She is!

HAROLD	I'm off!
	(He starts to run away, but CHARLIE grabs him and brings him back.)
CHARLIE	Now, Harold, you mustn't go dashing off like that. (To MRS. FLETCHER-BREWER.) He's very impetuous. (To HAROLD.) Anyone would think you had a guilty conscience.
CAROL	Don't you worry, Mr. Spook. My mother may be a J.P., but she's certainly not going to tell your wife where you are.
MRS. F-B	Good heavens, no! I wouldn't dream of spoiling her nice surprise. (Rising.) Come along, Carol. I think it's time we got ready for dinner.
HAROLD	(nudging her) Get away! You've only just 'ad tea!
CHARLIE	Harold!
	(MRS. FLETCHER-BREWER gives him a withering look.)
MRS. F-B	We have to make ourselves respectable.
HAROLD	Aye, that'll be a long job, won't it? (His smile dies as he sees MRS. FLETCHER-BREWER glaring at him.)
MRS. F-B	(to CAROL) Come along! I'm sure these gentlemen will excuse us.
HAROLD	Why? What have you done?
	(MRS. FLETCHER-BREWER gives him another cold look and goes off upstairs. CAROL smiles and follows her off. CHARLIE turns to HAROLD.)
CHARLIE	What are you trying to do? Get us both ninety-nine years?
HAROLD	Well, I wish I'd never come. (He sits down on the sofa and starts to eat some of the bread-and-butter.)
CHARLIE	You just don't know how to behave, that's your trouble. You're common, Spook. Common, common and silly.
HAROLD	(munching) H'm. This is quite nice.
CHARLIE	Well, don't eat the lot! (He sits beside HAROLD

and helps himself to bread-and-butter. There is a short pause as they enjoy the food.)   Fred'll be down in a minute.

HAROLD	Who?
CHARLIE	Fred Baxter. He'll be glad to see <u>you</u>.
HAROLD	Jam?
CHARLIE	Oh, thanks. (He takes it.)
HAROLD	Who's Fred Baxter?
CHARLIE	(confidentially) He's the brains behind the whole thing.
HAROLD	(impressed) Is he? Get away!
CHARLIE	You've got him to thank for being here.
HAROLD	Have I really?
CHARLIE	Of course. Jam?
HAROLD	(taking it) Oh, thanks.
CHARLIE	It was Baxter's brains and Baxter's money that got you off the hook, y'know.
HAROLD	Well, that was very nice of him. Hardly seems worth it, though, does it?
CHARLIE	What do you mean?
HAROLD	Well, I was coming out a week on Friday, anyway.
CHARLIE	(amused) A week on Friday? You must have lost count. You were there for seven more years if we hadn't got you out. (He takes a bite of bread-and-jam.)
HAROLD	Don't be daft! The wife was coming to the gate to meet me a week on Friday.
CHARLIE	(eating) No, Harold. Seven years on Friday. Even <u>you</u> couldn't have had that much good conduct! Now - this <u>was</u> the place, wasn't it?
HAROLD	Eh?
CHARLIE	Hook House Hotel - this <u>was</u> the place?

HAROLD	What place?
CHARLIE	(confidentially) Where you hid the money, of course!
HAROLD	I did?
CHARLIE	You and the other chap. The one who's still inside.
HAROLD	(smiling) Get away! I've never been 'ere before in me life!
CHARLIE	(trying to be patient) No, you haven't - but he has!
HAROLD	Who?

(CHARLIE gives a quick look around to make sure they are not being overheard.)

CHARLIE	Your partner! He stayed here and hid the stuff the night before you were both arrested. Now he's in the Isle of Wight.
HAROLD	What's he doing there?
CHARLIE	(impatiently) Well, he's not on holiday, is he?
HAROLD	Oh, what a shame! Nice for a holiday, is the Isle of Wight. I took the kids there once - Ventnor, it was -
CHARLIE	Harold! You're the only other person who knows where the money is. That's why we got you out.
HAROLD	Well, you've been wasting your time, 'aven't you? Looks as if you got the wrong one.
CHARLIE	(alarmed) The wrong one? You - you don't mean there were two of you in there?
HAROLD	Aye!
CHARLIE	Two Spooks in one prison?
HAROLD	Yes!
CHARLIE	Oh, my God!
HAROLD	He 'ad seven more years to do - I was coming out a week on Friday. I expect it was him you were after.

CHARLIE	(a shattered man) I don't believe it!
HAROLD	(chattily) I was a bit puzzled when I started getting all those messages - you know. But I didn't like to go to the other one and say, "Are these for you?" I mean, it might 'ave been a bit embarrassing, mightn't it?
CHARLIE	And when you were being shoved over the wall, didn't you think of saying, "I'm going out a week on Friday"?
HAROLD	Aye, I did!
CHARLIE	Well, what did they say?
HAROLD	They said, "Oh, no you're not - you're going out now!"
CHARLIE	But all the way down here you never mentioned it. You never said it was a mistake..
HAROLD	I didn't know what it was all about. Anyhow, I didn't get much chance to talk, did I? Trussed up in the boot like that.
CHARLIE	(a beaten man) So you - you don't know where the money is hidden?
HAROLD	Well, how could I? Fancy you thinking I was in there for armed robbery! (He chuckles.)
CHARLIE	Well, what <u>were</u> you in for?
	(HAROLD leans towards CHARLIE and whispers something in his ear. CHARLIE reacts.)
	Harold - you didn't!
HAROLD	Only once.
CHARLIE	Baxter 'll kill me when he finds out!
HAROLD	(cheerfully) Not if you tell him what happened. I mean, it was a natural mistake, wasn't it? I don't suppose you've done this sort of thing before, 'ave you?
CHARLIE	No, I haven't.
HAROLD	No, I thought not.
CHARLIE	I shall be dead before dinner. What are we going to do?
HAROLD	Well, I don't know about you, but I'm going back to

'ave a cup of tea with the Governor.

(He starts to go but CHARLIE restrains him.)

CHARLIE   Just a minute! You can't leave me like this - to be shot all on my own. It wouldn't be fair on Baxter.

HAROLD   Why not?

CHARLIE   He might want to shoot you, too.

HAROLD   What for? I haven't done nothing!

CHARLIE   He might not believe your story. I mean, we've only your word. He might think you were trying to keep all the money for yourself. No, there's only one thing for it - we'll have to search the whole place until we find it.

HAROLD   And what if we can't?

CHARLIE   Then we'll have to run!

HAROLD   I'd rather run now!

(HAROLD starts to run upstage, but as he does so FRED appears at the top of the stairs and comes down. HAROLD runs in the opposite direction, circles the sofa and ends up facing FRED U.C. He runs on the spot.)

FRED   You going somewhere?

HAROLD   Just for a bit of a run. Got to keep fit, you know! (He continues to run on the spot.)

FRED   Cut that out!

HAROLD   You what?

FRED   (loudly)   Cut it out!

(HAROLD stops running and begins to shake all over.)

Keep still.

HAROLD   I can't!

FRED   Not cold, are you?

HAROLD   No - not yet!

FRED   Then stop shivering!

(HAROLD gradually manages to control his shakes.)

'Ave you stopped?

HAROLD   Aye. I think so.

(FRED starts to move downstage. As he does so, HAROLD starts to shake again. FRED looks back and catches him. HAROLD stops shaking again and smiles weakly.)

Would you like some bread and jam?

(FRED looks at HAROLD and then turns to CHARLIE, not able to believe his eyes.)

FRED   Is this the man Spook?

CHARLIE   (nervously)   Er – yes.

FRED   Does he always look like that?

HAROLD   I told 'im he should 'ave got me a better suit.

FRED   Don't look much like a bank robber to me.

HAROLD   No, and as a matter of fact –

(CHARLIE kicks him on the ankle.)

'Ere!

CHARLIE   (putting a friendly arm around HAROLD's shoulders) You mustn't go by outside appearances. I know he doesn't look much now – after a long journey – but wait till you see him in the morning.

HAROLD   I won't be 'ere in the morning –

FRED   What's that?

CHARLIE   He means if everything goes according to plan.

FRED   You seem to 'ave forgotten the plan, Charlie boy. We wait until everyone's in bed, then we collect the stuff, have a good night's kip and leave to-morrow morning.

CHARLIE   Oh, yes – of course.

HAROLD   Suppose we can't find it?

FRED   (ominously)   What did you say?

HAROLD	Suppose we can't find the money.
FRED	'Aven't lost your memory, 'ave you, Spook?
HAROLD	No - it's just that - somebody might 'ave moved it -
FRED	There's only two people could do that, Spook. And one of 'em's still on the inside.
HAROLD	Oh, aye - in the Isle of Wight! (Innocently.) Who's the other one?
FRED	(coming close to HAROLD) Don't you know?
HAROLD	No.
FRED	Can't you 'azard a guess?
HAROLD	No.
FRED	I'll give you three tries.
HAROLD	(giggling) Nay, I'm no good at party games!
FRED	(loudly) You!
HAROLD	Me?
FRED	Yes!
HAROLD	No - I never touched it!
CHARLIE	No, of course he didn't. I mean, he hasn't had the chance, has he?
FRED	You'd better not 'ave done, Spook, because if you 'ave it'll mean you are trying to cut your friends out of their fair share - and we wouldn't like that, would we?
HAROLD	No!
FRED	If you 'ad done such a thing, you would regret it, Spook. You mark my words. If you 'ad double-crossed us, your name would become your nature, Spook - you'd be nothing but a plume of white floating up into the sky!
HAROLD	I - I never touched it!
CHARLIE	I know Spook. He's a good little chap. He wouldn't let us down.
FRED	(to HAROLD) Just you remember this. If it 'adn't

been for me and Charlie, you wouldn't be sitting 'ere in
a country 'otel casting your eye down the à la carte -
you'd be inside, 'aving full board during 'Er Majesty's
pleasure!

HAROLD   Aye, and I know which I'd rather be doing.

FRED   (turning on him again)   Well?

HAROLD   (weakening)   I'd rather be sitting here.

FRED   All right, then. Come over 'ere, 'Arold.

(Rather tentatively, HAROLD goes to FRED, who is
standing near the sofa.)

Would you like to sit down on the sofa?

HAROLD   Well, I -

FRED   (loudly)   Sit down on the sofa!

(HAROLD sits down with a rush. FRED sits beside him.
CHARLIE is standing on the other side.)

(Gently.)   Not frightened of me, are you, 'Arold?

HAROLD   No.

FRED   I'm your friend. Did you know that?

HAROLD   Are you?

FRED   Yes.

HAROLD   Oh.   (To CHARLIE.)   He's my friend.

CHARLIE   So there's nothing to be frightened of, is there?

HAROLD   No!   (He smiles happily.)

FRED   Now, 'Arold, I want you to concentrate. Put all
thoughts out of your 'ead.

CHARLIE   Go on, Harold. That can't be too difficult for you.
(He sits the other side of HAROLD on the sofa.)

FRED   Have you done that?

HAROLD   (closing his eyes)   Aye.

FRED   Now - cast your mind back.

HAROLD	Cast me mind back.
FRED	You done that?
HAROLD	(concentrating like mad) Aye.
FRED	Now - where did you 'ide the money?
HAROLD	(miserably) I don't know.
FRED	Spook!
HAROLD	Well, you told me to put all thoughts out of my 'ead!
FRED	Not all thoughts! Just the superfluous ones.
CHARLIE	All his thoughts are superfluous ones.
FRED	All right - we'll start again. You ready?
HAROLD	(closing his eyes) Aye.
FRED	Now - cast your mind back.
HAROLD	Cast me mind back -
FRED	Have you done that?
HAROLD	(dreamily) Aye -
FRED	You all ready now?
	(HAROLD, on the verge of sleep, gives a great yawn.)
	(Loudly.) Spook!
	(He shakes HAROLD, who wakes with a start.)
HAROLD	Is it time to get up?
FRED	Where did you put the money?
HAROLD	(unhappily) It's no good - I can't tell you! I don't know where it is!
FRED	Well, you'd better remember, 'adn't you? You 'ad better remember quick! Because to-night you are going to 'ave to produce that money!
	(NORAH comes in D.L.)
NORAH	Dinner 'll be ready soon. I'm just going to turn down your beds. (She makes for the stairs.)

HAROLD   (sensing an avenue of escape)   Wait a bit! I'll come and help you!

NORAH   (smiling)   You saucy rascal!

(HAROLD rises and runs quickly past her up the stairs. NORAH, beaming delightedly, races after him.)

Well, wait for me, then!   (She chases him off up the stairs.)

(FRED and CHARLIE burst out laughing, then suddenly realise that HAROLD is escaping and react.)

FRED   )
CHARLIE)   (together)   Spook!

And they are pursuing the others off as –

THE CURTAIN FALLS

ACT TWO

The same evening.

As the curtain rises, FRED is coming quickly down the stairs and CHARLIE is coming in from the front door. They meet C.

FRED	Did you find 'im?
CHARLIE	He's not in the outhouses.
FRED	How he gave us the slip I shall never know.
CHARLIE	Yes. It <u>was</u> extraordinary, wasn't it?
FRED	If you 'adn't tripped me up with your great feet we'd 'ave got 'im.
CHARLIE	I thought I had rather a neat foot. Size eight, narrow.
FRED	It was big enough to trip me up.
CHARLIE	(rather pleased) Yes, it did do that, didn't it?
	(CATCHPOLE comes in from the dining room in some distress.)
CATCHPOLE	Mr. Mullins! Mr. Baxter! You're breaking the cook's heart.
CHARLIE	Don't tell me the Brown Windsor's going off.
CATCHPOLE	You see, sir, this is her moment of glory. She likes to be appreciated at her peak.
CHARLIE	I'm not surprised. And now she's past it, you mean?
CATCHPOLE	Fadin' fast, sir. Fadin' fast.
FRED	Major, we 'ave worse things on our mind. Not likely you've 'ad sight nor sound of the man Spook?
CATCHPOLE	Not gone missing, has he?
FRED	Can't find 'im anywhere.
CATCHPOLE	You've searched high and low?
FRED	He ain't there.

CATCHPOLE	Then we have no alternative. (He crosses to the bar.)
FRED	What you going to do?
CATCHPOLE	Call the Police.
	(FRED and CHARLIE go quickly to him and bring him downstage again, one on each side.)
CHARLIE	Oh, no! There's no need for that!
CATCHPOLE	But if Mr. Spook is missing –
FRED	We never said he was missing.
CATCHPOLE	I must have misunderstood – I thought you said –
FRED	We said he wasn't 'ere.
CATCHPOLE	Exactly!
FRED	We didn't say he was missing.
CATCHPOLE	I don't quite –
CHARLIE	Well, he might be playing a joke, you see. He does that sometimes.
FRED	Yes. He's a very 'igh-spirited boy is Spook.
CATCHPOLE	Oh, I see. A bit of a wag, eh?
FRED	Yes. Quite a bit.
CHARLIE	So if he is playing a joke we don't want to bother the Police, do we?
CATCHPOLE	(coldly) In that case, sir, perhaps the game of hide-and-seek could wait until after dinner? Be a shame to break the cook's 'eart for the whim of a practical joker.
CHARLIE	Yes, of course. Come on, Fred. We must think of the cook's peak.
FRED	(not too keen) Er – yes – I suppose so.
CATCHPOLE	This way, then, gentlemen! (He starts to lead the way D.L.) By the way, I've put you at the table next to Mrs. Fletcher-Brewer.
CHARLIE	Good lord, have you? I mean – oh, yes, thank you.

(They all go off D.L. As soon as they have gone, the door D.R. opens and EDNA's head appears. She looks about to see that all is clear, then comes out and crosses quickly to the bar from behind which she collects a plate of ham salad and a knife and fork. As she turns to C., the cupboard door opens and HAROLD comes out. EDNA screams and drops the food.)

HAROLD   S'sh! It's only me!

(They go on hands and knees to collect up the food.)

What you want to go and make all that noise for?

EDNA   Well, I 'ardly expected you to come out of a cupboard, did I? You said you'd be in your room.

HAROLD   I 'ad to move or they'd 'ave found me.

CATCHPOLE   (off)   It's all right, Norah. I'll go and see for myself.

EDNA   Mr. Catchpole! Quick!

(HAROLD darts back into the cupboard and closes the door. CATCHPOLE comes in and sees EDNA standing motionless with the food. He crosses to her.)

CATCHPOLE   Was that you screaming?

EDNA   I thought I saw a mouse.

CATCHPOLE   What are you doin' standing' there with a plate of cold meat in your hand? Have you been stealin' from the kitchen?

EDNA   I'm entitled to my supper, ain't I? Same as anyone else.

CATCHPOLE   (with a superior smile)   We have rules here, Edna. Staff is to eat after residents, not during dinner. You don't find the waiters at the Savoy 'Otel stopping in the middle of serving the pâté de fois to take out a packet of Marmite sandwiches, do you?

EDNA   I was a bit peckish.

CATCHPOLE   Well, you can peck away as much as you like – after you've done the washing-up.

EDNA   Yes, Mr. Catchpole.   (She puts down the food and
              starts to go.)

CATCHPOLE   Edna!

              (She stops.)

              Don't leave the food here. We don't want to encourage
              the mice, do we? Leave that stuff lying about and
              before we know where we are you'll be blowin' a penny
              whistle and dancin' about in fancy knickers like the
              Pied Piper!

              (She collects the food and goes off D.L., followed by
              CATCHPOLE, shaking his head in despair. HAROLD
              comes out and looks about for the food, but cannot find
              it. Thinking she may have hidden it, he goes on to all
              fours to look under the sofa, etc. He is at the R. end
              of the sofa as NORAH comes in with a tray on which is
              a pot of coffee and a pot of milk, two cups and saucers
              and some lump sugar. She puts the tray down on the
              coffee table and then sees HAROLD. She smiles
              broadly. He is not yet aware of her presence. She
              moves round quietly to behind him.)

NORAH   Harold!

              (He jumps a mile and turns to see her beaming at him.)

HAROLD   Oh, 'eck!

NORAH   Thought you'd got away from me, eh? What you looking
              for down there?

HAROLD   Er – nothing!   (Rising hurriedly.)   I'd better be
              off –

NORAH   You're not going to disappear again, are you?
              (She advances.)   I'll be off duty in a few minutes –
              then we can 'ave a little get-together.

HAROLD   A little what?

NORAH   Just you and me. I'll meet you out the back – behind
              the pigsty.

HAROLD   But I'm married!

NORAH	So am I!
HAROLD	I've got a wife!
NORAH	Well, she's not 'ere, is she?
HAROLD	No, but your husband is!
	(He tries to get away but she grabs him. He is resisting as CHARLIE comes in D.L. He sees them and quickly closes the door.)
CHARLIE	Spook!
	(HAROLD and NORAH disentangle.)
	What's this? The cabaret?
NORAH	(gazing rapturously at HAROLD) I just can't resist 'im!
CHARLIE	You <u>must</u> be in a bad way. I think you're wanted in the dining-room.
NORAH	Has he missed me?
CHARLIE	I don't know, but he's breathing heavily and muttering in Chinese.
NORAH	Oo! I'd better go, then! I shan't be long. And don't you go 'iding yourself again! (She passes behind CHARLIE, gives him a quick pinch en route and goes out D.L.)
CHARLIE	(gently rubbing his behind) If I stay here much longer I shall be black and blue. Now, look here, Spook, I can't cover up for you much longer. If you keep popping out like a Jack-in-the-Box, Baxter's bound to find you.
HAROLD	Where is he now?
CHARLIE	In the middle of dinner.
HAROLD	<u>I</u> wanted some.
CHARLIE	You wouldn't have liked it. It's not what you're used to.
HAROLD	What was it, then?
CHARLIE	(off-hand) Oh, only onion soup, saddle of lamb

and green peas, ice cream with chocolate sauce -

HAROLD   (suffering)   Oh, I'm 'ungry!

CHARLIE   How can you be? I gave you a paste sandwich on the
                way down.   (He sees the coffee.)   I say, look!
                Here you are - the very thing - some coffee. That'll
                take away the pangs.   (He pours two cups of coffee.)

HAROLD   I want more than coffee.

CHARLIE   Don't be so ungrateful. You can't expect me to bring
                onion soup, saddle of lamb, green peas and ice cream
                with chocolate sauce out here to you. I mean, what
                would old Catchpole say if he met me in the doorway
                carrying a tray with onion soup, saddle of lamb, green
                peas and ice cream with chocolate sauce?

HAROLD   O-o-oh!   (He gulps down one cup of coffee.)

CHARLIE   Anyhow, after what you've been eating lately it would
                only have disagreed with you if you'd had onion soup,
                saddle of lamb, green peas and -

HAROLD   O-o-oh!   (He gulps down the second cup of coffee.)

CHARLIE   There! That's better, isn't it?

CATCHPOLE   (off)   You'll find coffee in the lounge, madam.

MRS. F-B   (off)   Thank you, Major Catchpole.

HAROLD   Somebody coming!

CHARLIE   Quick - back inside!

HAROLD   (making for the cupboard)   Will you get me some
                food?

CHARLIE   Oh, all right.   (He gets a handful of sugar lumps
                from the coffee tray.)   Here you are - that'll keep
                your strength up.   (He puts the lumps into his hands,
                pushes him inside and shuts the door.)

                (MRS. FLETCHER-BREWER and CAROL, now in dinner
                dresses, come in from the dining-room.)

MRS. F-B   You left very quickly, Mr. Mullins.

CHARLIE   I wanted a breath of air.

CAROL	(with a smile) In the middle of dinner?
CHARLIE	Oh, yes! You should try it. Awfully good for the digestion. (He makes for the door D.L.)
	(The ladies settle themselves on the sofa.)
MRS. F-B	Ah! Coffee!
CHARLIE	(nervously) What?
	(MRS. FLETCHER-BREWER tries to pour the coffee and discovers the pot to be empty. She looks puzzled and sighs wearily.)
MRS. F-B	Are you returning to the dining-room?
CHARLIE	Er - yes.
MRS. F-B	Would you inform Major Catchpole that I should like some coffee? Tell him that an empty pot is of no avail.
	(He stumbles out.)
	I don't know what's happening to this hotel. I shall write to the Automobile Association. Three stars is frankly fanciful! (She opens the evening paper.)
	(The cupboard door opens slowly and HAROLD peers out. CAROL sees him. He sees CAROL. He smiles weakly and waves to her. She smiles, raises her hand and gives a small wave in return. MRS. FLETCHER-BREWER lowers her paper and sees what CAROL is doing. CAROL attempts to cover up by adjusting her hair. Repeat the business. Again MRS. FLETCHER-BREWER lowers her newspaper and catches CAROL, who again tries to cover up.)
	Carol - what on earth is the matter with you?
CAROL	The matter, Mother?
MRS. F-B	Why all this ridiculous semaphore? You're behaving like a Girl Guide on an exercise.
	(HAROLD, disappearing into the cupboard, closes the door too quickly and the slam is clearly audible.)
	(Turning.) What was that?

CAROL	I didn't hear anything.
MRS. F-B	I distinctly heard a door bang.
CAROL	Perhaps the pigs have got out again.
	(Her mother gives her a doubtful look and returns to her newspaper.)
MRS. F-B	I see another of those wretched men has got out of prison.
CAROL	Not another?
MRS. F-B	He escaped early this morning. It really is quite scandalous the way these things are arranged from the outside.
CAROL	Is there any trace of him?
MRS. F-B	They seem to think he may have been heading in the direction of Crossley Green.
CAROL	But that's not far from here!
MRS. F-B	(ominously) Yes. I know.
	(CHARLIE comes in from D.L. with a packet of food behind his back.)
CHARLIE	Oh - still here? I mean - (He glances anxiously towards the cupboard.)
MRS. F-B	So to-night, Carol, we must be sure to lock our bedroom doors.
	(CHARLIE reacts, not having heard the previous conversation.)
CHARLIE	Oh, I'm sure that won't be necessary! (As MRS. FLETCHER-BREWER glares at him.) I mean - er - what I meant to say was - Oh, dear! What did I mean to say?
MRS. F-B	(brandishing the newspaper) It's all here in the evening paper!
CHARLIE	About locking your bedroom door?
MRS. F-B	About the man who got out!
CHARLIE	Ah! Too late locking your bedroom door!

MRS. F-B	About the man who got out of prison!
CHARLIE	Is it? Good lord!
MRS. F-B	This morning.
CHARLIE	I thought you said it was the _evening_ paper?
MRS. F-B	He got out this morning.
CHARLIE	There isn't a photograph, is there?
MRS. F-B	No.
CHARLIE	That's a relief.
MRS. F-B	What did you say?
CHARLIE	I can't bear those pictures, can you? So misleading. They always seem to look like someone you know.
	(CATCHPOLE comes in with a fresh pot of coffee.)
CATCHPOLE	More coffee, madam.
MRS. F-B	No.
CATCHPOLE	Madam?
MRS. F-B	Not _more_ coffee, Major.
CATCHPOLE	Oh. My mistake. (He starts to go out again.)
MRS. F-B	Bring it here!
CATCHPOLE	But I thought you said –
MRS. F-B	I should like some coffee!
CATCHPOLE	Er – yes, madam. (Somewhat bemused, he brings the coffee to her and starts to pour it out.)
CAROL	We were just talking about the prisoner who escaped this morning. It says in the evening paper that he may be in this area.
CATCHPOLE	Don't you worry about that, miss. I still have my old Service revolver.
CHARLIE	(alarmed) Have you?
CATCHPOLE	I like to keep it handy, sir. With a few rounds of ammunition, of course.

CHARLIE   Yes, of course.

CATCHPOLE   So don't you worry, ladies. If anybody starts prowling
               about here to-night, I shall let him have it — thick and
               fast!   (He goes out D.L.)

CHARLIE   I think he would, too.   (To CAROL.)   I hope
               you don't walk in your sleep.   (He glances
               anxiously towards the cupboard.)   Wouldn't you
               like to sit down?

MRS. F—B   Mr. Mullins, we are already sitting down.

CHARLIE   Ah, but in there!   (Indicating the door D.R.)

MRS. F—B   Are you hiding something?

CHARLIE   I beg your pardon?

MRS. F—B   Behind your back! Behind your back!

               (He looks behind his back, seems rather surprised and
               brings the package of food into view.)

CHARLIE   Oh, this? Yes. Well, I – I wrapped up a few odds and
               ends. I hoped you wouldn't be here.

MRS. F—B   What?

CHARLIE   I mean – in the middle of the night I might feel a bit
               peckish. You never know what you're going to feel like
               in the middle of the night.   (To CAROL.)
               What do you feel like in the middle of the night?

MRS. F—B   Mr. Mullins!

CHARLIE   I beg your pardon.   (Another quick glance towards
               HAROLD's hiding place.)   I don't know why you're
               both sitting here.

CAROL   What do you mean?

CHARLIE   Well – it's not a very comfortable sofa.

MRS. F—B   I find it perfectly satisfactory.

CHARLIE   The moment I came into this hotel and clapped eyes on
               that sofa, I said to myself, "That sofa is uncomfortable".

CAROL   (with a smile)   What are you talking about?

CHARLIE	I'm only thinking of you. How do you think I feel, standing here watching you sit on that uncomfortable sofa?
CAROL	Are you trying to get rid of us?
CHARLIE	Yes! No!
CAROL	Then why are you going on about the sofa?
CHARLIE	I wouldn't be going on about it if it wasn't uncomfortable.
MRS. F-B	But it is comfortable!

(CHARLIE crosses purposefully to them.)

CHARLIE	Excuse me.

(The astonished ladies get up. He sits down and starts to bounce on it gently.)

Terrible! You can feel the springs.

CAROL	I didn't notice.
CHARLIE	Come and try!

(CAROL sits beside him and tries it. They bounce together for a while.)

There you are, you see!

(Exasperated, MRS. FLETCHER-BREWER goes and sits the other side of CHARLIE. She tries the sofa and then slowly starts to bounce. CHARLIE and CAROL join in, and all three are bouncing on the sofa when EDNA comes in D.L. She gazes, astonished, at the three of them, crosses slowly without taking her eyes off them, collects the tray of coffee things and goes out again, without speaking. The bouncing stops.)

MRS. F-B	It seems perfectly all right to me.
CHARLIE	But have you tried the ones in the television room?
MRS. F-B	Yes, but -
CHARLIE	Much more comfortable!
MRS. F-B	Mr. Mullins, have you been drinking? Come along, Carol. Let's take our coffee into the other room.

(She looks for the coffee.)   Now where's it got to?
Oh, really!   (She stomps off into the room D.R.)

(CAROL, following her, pauses at the door.)

CAROL   If you're looking for your friend, he's in the cupboard.
                 (She smiles and goes out.)

                 (CHARLIE reacts, then goes quickly to the cupboard and
                 taps on the door.)

CHARLIE   (in a whisper)   Spook.   (There is no reply.)
                 Spook!   (Again nothing, so he pulls open the door.)
                 All right. You can come out now.   (He stands back,
                 but nothing happens, so he looks inside the cupboard.)
                 Spook!   (He reacts. There is nobody inside.)
                 Good lord!   (He looks inside again.)   Come on.
                 Don't mess about. You must be in there somewhere.
                 Spook!   (He goes into the cupboard, leaving the
                 door open.)

                 (No sooner has he disappeared than CATCHPOLE comes
                 in D.L. He goes towards the bar, notices that the
                 cupboard is open and promptly closes the door and
                 fastens the catch. He then continues to the bar. He is
                 pouring a brandy as EDNA creeps in from L. with a
                 plate of salad. She does not see CATCHPOLE in the
                 corner behind the bar, and tiptoes carefully towards the
                 cupboard. When she gets nearly to it, he speaks.)

CATCHPOLE   Edna!

                 (She jumps a mile and drops the plate of salad on to the
                 ground.)

EDNA   You didn't 'alf give me a fright, Mr. Catchpole.

CATCHPOLE   What do you expect? Creeping in here like a thief in
                 the night.

EDNA   Look what you made me do! Now you've got coleslaw
                 all over your Kosset.   (She kneels down to pick up
                 the salad.)

CATCHPOLE   I don't know what's got into you, Edna. Every time I
                 look at you, you seem to 'ave a plate of 'am salad in

	your 'and. You suffering from night starvation?
EDNA	I dunno what you mean.
CATCHPOLE	(suddenly struck by the thought) Here! You haven't got somebody 'idden away, have you?
EDNA	No! No, of course not!
CATCHPOLE	Because there's people at large, you know.
EDNA	People?
CATCHPOLE	At large.
EDNA	What sort of people?
CATCHPOLE	Ruthless people. The criminal classes, you understand? And if you was to take plates of 'am salad to one of them sort, there's no knowing what would happen to you. So for God's sake keep your eyes peeled and your 'ands off of the grub! (He takes the plate of salad from her and sweeps out D.L.)
	(EDNA stands for a moment, undecided, then she sees the package of food which CHARLIE has left on the coffee table. She looks inside and sees the food.)
EDNA	Well, I never!
	(She takes the food to the cupboard, unfastens the catch and opens the door. CHARLIE walks out. She screams, drops the food and races off D.L. CHARLIE closes the cupboard door and is picking up the food as MRS. FLETCHER–BREWER appears at the door D.R.)
MRS. F–B	Was that you, Mr. Mullins?
CHARLIE	Was what me?
MRS. F–B	Screaming. Was it you?
CHARLIE	It wasn't in here. It must have been out there. I expect it was the pigs.
MRS. F–B	It sounded human.
CHARLIE	I can't help that.
MRS. F–B	I see you are already feeling peckish.

CHARLIE	What? (Reacting to the food.) Oh, yes.
	(She goes off, and CATCHPOLE appears from the bar door.)
CATCHPOLE	Who was that?
CHARLIE	Mrs. Fletcher-Brewer.
CATCHPOLE	Screaming?
CHARLIE	I expect she's over-excited. You know what these television programmes are like.
CATCHPOLE	Ah - yes! (He goes out again.)
	(As soon as the bar door closes, the one D.L. opens and FRED comes in.)
FRED	Anybody about?
CHARLIE	They're in there.
FRED	What about Spook?
CHARLIE	Still no sign of him. (Truthfully.) I can't think where he's got to.
FRED	You 'ad a good look?
CHARLIE	A very good look.
FRED	What about the cupboard?
CHARLIE	It's empty.
FRED	You sure?
CHARLIE	Unless he's turned into a broom.
FRED	Let's 'ave another look.
CHARLIE	You're wasting your time.
	(FRED opens the cupboard door and HAROLD comes out. FRED glares at CHARLIE. CHARLIE cannot believe his eyes.)
CHARLIE	He wasn't there a moment ago.
FRED	What did he do, then? Disappear down his own earhole? (He turns to HAROLD.) All right, Spook, you tell

	us. How did you manage to spirit yourself away?
HAROLD	There's another door at the other end.
FRED	'Ow convenient! Where does it lead to?
HAROLD	The wine cellar! (He produces a bottle of wine from behind his back.)
FRED	'Ow dare you drink when you're on duty? (He takes the bottle.)
HAROLD	Can I go now?
	(He starts to go, but FRED grabs him.)
FRED	Go, Spook? Go empty-'anded? 'Ave you forgotten what you're 'ere for?
HAROLD	(miserably) But I told you - I don't know where the money is!
FRED	Now, Spook, you want to see me 'appy, don't you?
HAROLD	Aye.
FRED	You want to see me smile, don't you?
HAROLD	Aye.
FRED	You wouldn't want to upset me, would you?
HAROLD	(warmly) No.
FRED	Then you'd better start thinking, or by the morning a man in a black 'at and a long coat will be coming for you with a box!
HAROLD	What will I want a box for?
FRED	(to CHARLIE) I can't think how he even got into 'Er Majesty's Prison - never mind out of it! All right, Charlie boy, let's 'ave a look at the register. Look up March fourteenth. See what room old Spook's friend stayed in. Maybe he 'id the stuff in 'is bedroom.
	(CHARLIE goes to the bar and thumbs through the register. HAROLD has seen the package of food and is examining the contents happily. FRED sees him.)
	What you doing?

HAROLD	I thought I'd have a bite to eat.
FRED	This is no time for food. We've got work to do.
HAROLD	But I 'aven't 'ad my dinner yet!
FRED	There's a time and a place to eat, and the time isn't now and the place isn't 'ere! You might 'ave to move quickly. We don't want you crawling about the place all 'eavy with calories. (He takes the food and puts it on the bar.)
CHARLIE	Here we are!
FRED	You got it?
CHARLIE	Yes. Poplar.
FRED	Poplar? Don't be daft! That's where he comes from.
CHARLIE	No, no! That's the name of his room. The tree Poplar.
FRED	Oh. Well, who's in Poplar now?
	(CHARLIE turns the pages of the register.)
HAROLD	Couldn't I just 'ave one little mouthful?
FRED	When this is all over, Spook, you can retire to your room and 'ave smoked salmon and dancing girls sent up to you. But until that 'appy time you will do without. I don't want anything to interfere with the pitiful process going on inside your cranium.
HAROLD	What process?
FRED	Thinking!
CHARLIE	Here we are - Poplar!
FRED	Who's booked in there now?
CHARLIE	Mrs. Fletcher-Brewer.
FRED	She would be, wouldn't she? Don't suppose she's likely to 'ave left 'er door open.
CHARLIE	Not a hope. (He looks at the key rack behind the bar.) She's hung on to her key, as well.
FRED	You any good at picking locks, Spook?

HAROLD	(outraged) Here! What do you take me for?
FRED	All right, all right! Don't you look so innocent. You weren't inside for pinching the cream off the milk, remember.
CHARLIE	She's the outdoor type. Fishing and all that. She's probably left her window open.
FRED	To let the fresh air in.
CHARLIE	Only the fresh air would want to get in.
FRED	There's only one thing for it. Someone'll 'ave to climb up the wall and get in that way.
CHARLIE	Yes. But who?
	(They both turn and look at HAROLD. He smiles back, unsuspecting, then realises the implication.)
HAROLD	No! Not me!
CHARLIE	Harold, you must be reasonable. Fred and I have both had big dinners. You know - onion soup, saddle of lamb, green peas and ice cream with chocolate sauce.
HAROLD	(joining in) - green peas, and ice cream with chocolate sauce!
CHARLIE	Exactly! So, naturally, we're a little on the heavy side. It wouldn't be good for the digestion to go climbing about the place. You must see that.
FRED	So you see, Spook, 'ow lucky it is that you didn't eat anything.
CHARLIE	(to HAROLD) Right - we're all agreed, then. You're the one to do the job.
HAROLD	What job?
CHARLIE	Do pay attention! Up the wall and in through Mrs. Fletcher-Brewer's window.
HAROLD	(horrified) Up the wall?
CHARLIE	Yes.
HAROLD	Outside?

CHARLIE	Of course. That should be easy for you. After all, you had a bit of practice this morning. And that was a <u>big</u> wall. This one should be child's play.
HAROLD	I won't do it!
FRED	(gently) That's where you're wrong, Spook. You think you won't. You hope you won't. But when it comes to it, you'll surprise yourself.
CHARLIE	You'll go up that wall like a mountain goat.
HAROLD	Suppose somebody sees me?
CHARLIE	It's dark. Besides, there's nobody out there.
HAROLD	Suppose Mrs. Fletcher-Brewer's in her room? I can't just climb in through her bedroom window and expect her to ignore me.
FRED	Tell 'er you're cleaning the windows.
HAROLD	At this time of night?
FRED	Oh, for 'eaven's sake, she's in there – watching the telly!
HAROLD	How do I know she'll stay there?
FRED	You don't. But where's your spirit of adventure?
HAROLD	I 'aven't got one!
FRED	Well, you'd better find one quick, 'cos you're going to need it.
CHARLIE	Don't worry, Harold. If she comes out of there we'll head her off.
HAROLD	You mean – you'll both be in 'ere?
CHARLIE	Yes.
HAROLD	Sitting 'ere?
CHARLIE	Yes.
HAROLD	In the bar?
CHARLIE	Yes.
HAROLD	Having a drink?

CHARLIE	We might.
HAROLD	(aggrieved) While I'm out there climbing up the wall?
CHARLIE	Well, somebody's got to do the dull part!
FRED	Now - once you're inside search the place from top to bottom. That money must be there somewhere.
CHARLIE	But make sure you leave everything as you found it. We don't want her suspecting anything.
HAROLD	Do I 'ave to climb back down the wall again?
CHARLIE	No, you fool! Make sure no-one's about, then come out by the door.
FRED	Now, come on, Spook! While the coast is clear.
HAROLD	But how do I get up the wall?
FRED	(wearily) Use your imagination!
HAROLD	How can I climb on that?
FRED	The ivy, Spook! The ivy! Pull yourself up the ivy!
	(They hustle him towards the front door.)
	And Spook - !
HAROLD	Aye?
FRED	If you come back empty-'anded, don't expect to find me smiling.
	(They push HAROLD out and close the door. They move downstage, but as they go the front door opens and HAROLD re-appears.)
HAROLD	'Ere! I don't know which is her room!
	(They go to him quickly.)
CHARLIE	Round the back. First floor. Second window along. Right?
HAROLD	Second window. Right.
	(They push him out again, close the door and move down-stage.)

FRED	I 'ope we 'aven't made a mistake leaving Spook to do the dirty work.
CHARLIE	Well, I'd be no good. I've never climbed up ivy in my life.
	(NORAH comes in D.L. She has taken off her apron and is carrying her coat.)
NORAH	Is he waiting?
CHARLIE	What?
NORAH	For me. I said I'd meet 'im later, back of the pigsty. (She makes for the front door, pulling on her coat.)
	(CHARLIE and FRED stop her.)
CHARLIE	No, no! He's not out there!
NORAH	Where is he, then? I don't want to keep 'im waiting.
CHARLIE	He left here a moment ago. Just before you came in. He was standing here and he went.
NORAH	Where?
CHARLIE	Definitely.
NORAH	But where definitely?
CHARLIE	Fred, where did he go definitely?
FRED	He said he was going upstairs.
CHARLIE	Yes, that's right!
NORAH	Then he should be there by now.
CHARLIE	If he's clinging on all right.
NORAH	Clinging on?
CHARLIE	To the banisters. They're very steep stairs for a little chap like him.
NORAH	I'll go and see 'ow he's getting on.
	(She starts to go, but they each take an arm and bring her downstage again.)
FRED	No!

CHARLIE	You don't want to be standing out there in the cold, with the pigs grunting all over the place. I tell you what – why don't you meet him inside?
NORAH	In 'ere? I couldn't do that!
CHARLIE	No, not in here. But you see this cupboard –
NORAH	(with a little laugh) I can't meet 'im in a cupboard!
CHARLIE	No, but at the other end of the cupboard there's a door leading to the wine cellar.
NORAH	Yes, I know!
CHARLIE	You wait in there – and we'll send him to you.
NORAH	(surprised and delighted) Would you?
CHARLIE	Of course!
NORAH	Oo! You are wicked!
	(She is about to pinch him again, but he quickly side-steps to avoid it.)
CHARLIE	Ah-ha!
NORAH	I'll do it! (She goes up to the cupboard and opens the door.)
	(FRED picks up the bottle of wine and gives it to her.)
FRED	'Ere you are. Take this with you. That'll warm you up a bit.
NORAH	I don't need any warming up!
	(She pinches CHARLIE on the bottom and goes into the cupboard. They close the door after her. CATCHPOLE comes running in from D.L.)
CATCHPOLE	I say! There's someone outside!
CHARLIE	Outside?
CATCHPOLE	Climbin' up the creeper!
FRED	You must be mistaken.
CATCHPOLE	I saw 'im with my own eyes! There's people at large, and one of 'em's half-way up the ivy!

CHARLIE	What sort of people?
CATCHPOLE	Them as should be inside is outside.
CHARLIE	(quietly) Well, I wish he'd hurry up and get inside.
CATCHPOLE	The criminal classes is on the march!
FRED	I thought you said there was only one of them?
CATCHPOLE	Yes - outside - swinging from the side of the 'ouse like Tarzan of the Apes! But there'll be others skulking in the bushes! (He races for the stairs.)
CHARLIE	Where are you going?
CATCHPOLE	To get my old Service revolver.
CHARLIE	But you might hurt somebody!
CATCHPOLE	Hurt somebody? I'm going to kill somebody! (He races off up the stairs.)
CHARLIE	What are we going to do? He's going to get a gun and shoot Spook.
FRED	Well, that'll save me the trouble.
CHARLIE	He's going to pick him off like a duck at a fairground. I'd better go and warn him. (He goes towards the front door.)
FRED	The bloody fool! He should 'ave been inside by now. What's he 'anging about out there for?
CHARLIE	I'll ask him. (He goes out.)
	(MRS. FLETCHER-BREWER comes in D.R. from the television room.)
MRS. F-B	What on earth is going on?
FRED	Nothing's going on.
MRS. F-B	Nothing going on? Everybody shouting like a football match and you tell me nothing's going on?
FRED	Oh, that! That was old Catchpole.
MRS. F-B	Not like the Major to shout.
FRED	He's been 'aving words with the cook.

MRS. F-B	What words?
FRED	I couldn't repeat them in front of a lady.
	(CHARLIE bursts in.)
CHARLIE	It's all right! He's inside! (He sees MRS. FLETCHER-BREWER.) I say, you're missing the telly!
MRS. F-B	I came out because of the noise.
CHARLIE	Well, turn the volume down.
MRS. F-B	The noise out here!
CHARLIE	Did you hear any noise, Fred?
FRED	Only Catchpole and the cook.
CHARLIE	The cook?
FRED	You remember the cook.
CHARLIE	Oh, yes. Her mother's got terrible legs.
MRS. F-B	This place is fast becoming a madhouse. I shall go to bed.
	(She makes for the stairs but they quickly intercept her.)
CHARLIE	No! You can't do that!
MRS. F-B	Can't, Mr. Mullins? Can't?
CHARLIE	Your room isn't ready yet.
MRS. F-B	Not?
CHARLIE	Decidedly not.
FRED	There's somebody in there.
MRS. F-B	What?
FRED	Yes - the maid - turning down the bed.
CHARLIE	You wouldn't want to go marching into your room and find somebody turning down your bed, would you?
MRS. F-B	They will doubtless have gone by the time I get upstairs!
CHARLIE	(quietly) I hope so.

MRS. F—B	What did you say?
CHARLIE	I said I should jolly well hope so. You can't have maids hanging about turning down beds.
MRS. F—B	I shall not disturb them.
	(She makes another move but again they stop her.)
FRED	But it's the staff, you see.
MRS. F—B	The staff?
FRED	Yes – they're very touchy.
CHARLIE	Only last week two maids left because somebody caught them turning down the beds.
FRED	It's a job they prefer to do unseen.
CHARLIE	You can't blame them, really. How would you like to have someone standing behind you on the Bench?
	(They escort her, one on each side, back to the door D.R.)
	So if you'll just be patient –
FRED	For about five minutes –
CHARLIE	And sit down in here –
FRED	By the time you go upstairs –
CHARLIE	Everything will be ready for you!
MRS. F—B	Oh, really!
	(They push her gently into the television room and close the door as CATCHPOLE races down the stairs, carrying his Service revolver.)
CATCHPOLE	You get on the telephone – ring the Police! I'll go and apprehend him! (He turns at the door.) Lucky I kept this thing handy, eh? (He goes out the front door, closing it after him.)
CHARLIE	Come on – quick! We've got to get old Spook out of that bedroom!
	(He runs off upstairs with FRED following him. The front

door opens slowly and POLLY and MR. PARKINSON
come in. She is about 26, blonde, with a good figure.
She speaks with a Cockney accent and is wearing a smart
raincoat over a blouse and skirt, and perilously high
heels. Her father, MR. PARKINSON, is very old,
vague, rather deaf and walks with a degree of uncertainty.
POLLY carries two small suitcases which she puts down
near the door. They then come down to C., looking
about.)

POLLY   This must be the place, Dad.

MR. P.   Eh? What—you—say?

POLLY   The place we're looking for! This must be it.

MR. P.   I'd say this was the place.

POLLY   (patiently)   Yes, Dad. Not much sign of life.

MR. P.   What d'you expect? I'm an old man.

POLLY   Not you – this place. Looks 'alf dead.

MR. P.   I'm not surprised after that walk up from the station.

POLLY   You sit down, Dad, eh? Have a little rest while I find
out about our rooms.

MR. P.   I think I'd rather have a little rest.   (He sits in the
armchair near the fire.)

               (POLLY rings the bell at the bar. MR. PARKINSON
discovers the package of food on the chair, opens it and
starts to eat.)

POLLY   Well, I hope it's going to be worth it. Coming all this
way.

MR. P.   Why'd you bring me here? I'd have been better off at
home.

POLLY   I couldn't come and stay here all on my own, now could
I? People might 'ave got the wrong idea. Nobody
answering that bell. I'll go and see if I can find anyone.
(She goes off D.L.)

               (MR. PARKINSON munches slowly and contentedly.
CATCHPOLE runs in from the front door.)

CATCHPOLE	There's no sign of him! He must have got inside!
	(He does not notice the stranger in the armchair and goes off quickly up the stairs. The old man is oblivious of the interruption and goes on steadily eating. MRS. FLETCHER-BREWER appears at the door D.R.)
MRS. F-B	Do you suppose I can now go to my bedroom alone? (She reacts, thinking nobody is there.) Huh! (She goes off again.)
	(The old man continues to eat. FRED and CHARLIE come down the stairs.)
CHARLIE	It was your fault! You shouldn't have banged on the bedroom door like that.
FRED	I was trying to warn 'im!
CHARLIE	Warn him? You scared him off! He thought it was Mrs. Fletcher-Brewer.
FRED	Well, he didn't 'ave to go climbing out of the window again, did he?
CHARLIE	There was no other way out! Come on, quick – before he leaves go of the ivy and breaks his bloody neck!
	(They go out through the front door, not having seen MR. PARKINSON and he not having seen them. POLLY comes back with EDNA.)
EDNA	Cleaning and general is what I do. Bookings is out of my province.
POLLY	Well, you're the only person I can find.
EDNA	Don't you raise your voice at me. (Seeing MR. PARKINSON.) Here! What's that you've left there?
POLLY	That's my Dad!
EDNA	I thought it was a bundle of washing.
POLLY	Now, look 'ere, we've 'ad a long journey, so don't you chance your luck! If you don't do bookings, who does?
EDNA	All the rooms is occupied.

POLLY	Now, look —
EDNA	I'm off duty and not to be interfered with!
	(From outside there is a loud cry from HAROLD as he falls off the ivy.)
POLLY	What was that?
EDNA	(calmly) Sounded like somebody falling off the ivy.
MR. P.	Anybody like a sandwich?
POLLY	Hadn't you better go and see?
EDNA	No point. They'll 'ave 'it the ground by now.
	(CATCHPOLE comes down the stairs.)
CATCHPOLE	I heard a cry!
EDNA	It wasn't me.
POLLY	It came from outside.
CATCHPOLE	Who are you?
	(He reaches the foot of the stairs and POLLY sees the gun in his hand. She screams and raises her hands. MRS. FLETCHER-BREWER and CAROL come in D.R.)
MRS. F-B	Major Catchpole! Why are you carrying firearms?
CATCHPOLE	It's him, madam!
MRS. F-B	Him?
CATCHPOLE	The one we were talkin' about. He's outside now!
MRS. F-B	Then I trust you have the safety catch off!
CATCHPOLE	He's just fallen off the ivy!
	(The front door opens and CHARLIE and FRED come in, supporting a groaning HAROLD. They bring him to C.)
CHARLIE	Oh, do be quiet, Harold! We caught you, didn't we?
CATCHPOLE	Mr. Spook! You mean it was _you_ out there climbin' on the ivy?
HAROLD	(miserably) Aye.

CHARLIE	(forcing a laugh)　　All part of the game!
MRS. F-B	Game, Mr. Mullins?
CHARLIE	Hide and seek.
CATCHPOLE	But I might have shot you!
FRED	Yes. Pity you didn't. Come on, 'Arold - over 'ere.
	(CHARLIE and FRED settle HAROLD down on the sofa to recover his composure.)
MRS. F-B	(finding CATCHPOLE's gun rather too near to her) Major, you had better put away that gun before somebody gets hurt.
CATCHPOLE	Oh, I beg your pardon, madam!　　　(He puts the gun away in his pocket.)
MRS. F-B	And now - if these gentlemen have quite finished playing games - perhaps we can all retire for the night.
CHARLIE	What a good idea!
MRS. F-B	I trust there will be no further disturbances! Come, Carol!
	(She marches off upstairs with CAROL following obediently. POLLY, who has been looking at HAROLD thoughtfully ever since he came in, now moves towards him.)
POLLY	'Ere! Haven't I seen you somewhere before?
	(HAROLD looks at her and reacts with horror as he recognises her.)
HAROLD	No!
	(CHARLIE and FRED look at him accusingly.)
CHARLIE) FRED　　)	(together)　　Harold!
HAROLD	No - you must be mistaking me for someone else! I've got a very common face.
FRED	You can say that again.
POLLY	I could have sworn I'd seen you somewhere.

CATCHPOLE	(to POLLY) Who are you, anyhow? What are you doing here, and who is that person?
POLLY	That's my Dad, and we're staying the night!
CATCHPOLE	Oh, no, you ain't. All the rooms is occupied.
POLLY	You don't think I'm going to drag him all the way back to London to-night, do you?
CATCHPOLE	The only thing we have left is the box-room.
POLLY	Well, that's all right. That'll do for 'im.
MR. P.	I'm not sleeping in no box.
POLLY	I didn't say you were -
MR. P.	I'll be sleeping in a box soon enough without starting now.
POLLY	(loudly) You're not sleeping in a box, Dad!
MR. P.	No, I'm not!
POLLY	That's what I said.
CATCHPOLE	(at the register) Right, then. He'll be in Privet. (He writes the entry.)
POLLY	You mean private.
CATCHPOLE	No - privet. All the rooms is named after trees.
POLLY	Privet's not a tree! It's only a hedge.
CATCHPOLE	Exactly - and that's only the box-room.
POLLY	(turning to her father) You 'ear that, Dad? You'll be in Privet.
MR. P.	They're not putting me out in the garden on a cold night like this!
CHARLIE	No, no - that's the box-room.
POLLY	They're all full up.
MR. P.	I'm not surprised if they've got boxes in 'em!
POLLY	There aren't any boxes, Dad. It's just called the box-room, but there aren't any boxes in it.

MR. P.   It's a bloody silly name, then, isn't it?

POLLY   (to CATCHPOLE)   Okay, then. That's him fixed.
                Now – whose bed am I going to sleep in?   (She
                looks around at them all.)

CHARLIE   Shall we draw lots?

POLLY   What? No volunteers?

CATCHPOLE   I'll have a word with the kitchen staff. Perhaps they can
                squeeze you in somewhere.   (He crosses D.L.)

POLLY   And while they're at it perhaps they can squeeze us
                something to eat.

CATCHPOLE   It's rather late for eating.

POLLY   Now, look – !

CATCHPOLE   But I'll see what I can do.   (He goes out D.L.)

POLLY   Come on, Dad!

MR. P.   Are we going home already?

POLLY   No! We're going to eat!

MR. P.   Well, it's about time.   (He goes out after CATCH-
                POLE.)

                (POLLY pauses in the doorway and looks back at
                HAROLD.)

POLLY   I could 'ave sworn I'd seen you somewhere.   (She
                goes out and closes the door.)

                (CHARLIE and FRED turn immediately on HAROLD.)

CHARLIE   All right, Harold – who is she?

HAROLD   I've never seen 'er before in me life.

FRED   You expect us to believe that? You jumped right out of
                your birthday suit as soon as you set eyes on 'er!

HAROLD   I – I thought it was someone else.

FRED   Who? Your long-lost mother?

HAROLD   Nay! My mother's older than that.

CHARLIE	Who did you think it was then? The prison Governor?
HAROLD	(clutching at straws) Aye!
FRED	Don't you play around with us, Spook!
CHARLIE	(gently) You can tell us. After all, we are your friends.
HAROLD	Are you?
CHARLIE	Well, don't sound so doubtful. Just look what we've done for you.
HAROLD	Aye! You've landed me 'ere for a start!
FRED	And that wasn't easy.
CHARLIE	If it hadn't been for us, just think what could have happened to you. We stopped you from breaking your neck when you fell off the ivy.
HAROLD	And who made me climb up the ivy?
FRED	Never mind that! We saved you from certain death. And what thanks do we get? None! Instead, you sit there on the sofa, secretive and smug.
CHARLIE	And one thing I can't stand is a smug Spook.
FRED	Come on, 'Arold – the truth!
CHARLIE	You have seen her before, haven't you?
HAROLD	(miserably) Aye.
CHARLIE	A bit of your murky past, eh?
HAROLD	No!
CHARLIE	When did you know her, then?
HAROLD	I didn't say I knew her, I said I'd seen her.
FRED	Where?
HAROLD	In prison.
CHARLIE	Inside?
HAROLD	Yes.
FRED	(sarcastically) I suppose she was a prison warder?

HAROLD	Get away! They don't 'ave women warders!
FRED	You surprise me. What was she doing there, then?
HAROLD	She was visiting.
CHARLIE	Oh, I see!
HAROLD	She 'ad a boy friend inside.
FRED	Oh, my God! That's all we need! Do you think she's liable to remember where she saw you?
HAROLD	She might.
CHARLIE	Then we really <u>will</u> be in the soup!

(EDNA comes in D.L. with some sheets and blankets.)

EDNA	I ought to 'ave a union, that's what I ought to 'ave, a union.
CHARLIE	Oh? Who with?
EDNA	A union to protect my rights. I'm being took advantage of, that's what.
CHARLIE	By whom?
EDNA	By 'im! That one my sister married. I came 'ere with strict understandings what's now being abused.
CHARLIE	Did you hear that, Fred? Someone's abusing her understandings.
EDNA	(to HAROLD) You'll 'ave to move off of there. I've got to make a bed on that.
FRED	You're not going to sleep there, are you?
EDNA	Not me. I'll be sleeping in my quarters, where I trust I'll 'ave no interference.
CHARLIE	Shall we take a vote on that?
FRED	Who you making the bed for, then?
EDNA	That young woman. The one that's just arrived. (She busies herself making the bed.)

(FRED takes CHARLIE on one side.)

FRED	We can't 'ave 'er sleeping down 'ere! How we going to search the place?
CHARLIE	Oh, yes - I'd forgotten that! (To EDNA.) Aren't there any other rooms?
EDNA	Only the box-room, and her father's sleeping there. She says he's too old for sleeping on sofas.
FRED	(to CHARLIE) We'll 'ave to think of something.
	(FRED and CHARLIE turn in unison to look at HAROLD.)
FRED) CHARLIE)	(together) Harold!
HAROLD	It's nothing to do with me -
CHARLIE	We can't let the young lady sleep down here, can we?
HAROLD	Why not?
CHARLIE	A pretty girl like that. It wouldn't be right.
HAROLD	Well, what am I supposed to do about it?
	(CATCHPOLE comes in from D.L.)
CATCHPOLE	You getting on with that bed, Edna?
EDNA	Well, I'm not milking the pigs, am I?
CATCHPOLE	There's no call for vulgarity.
EDNA	Well, why don't you open your bleedin'eyes? (She crosses below him to D.L.)
CATCHPOLE	Where you going?
EDNA	Can't sleep without a pillow, can she? (She bangs out and slams the door.)
CATCHPOLE	(turning to the others) She's very 'ighly-strung.
CHARLIE	I wondered why she gave up playing the piano.
	(MRS. FLETCHER-BREWER appears from upstairs, about to erupt.)
MRS. F-B	Somebody has been rummaging in my drawers!
CATCHPOLE	Rummaging, Mrs. Fletcher-Brewer?

MRS. F-B	Rummaging, Major Catchpole! They have disarranged my dresses, and tampered with my toilet water!
FRED	(aside to HAROLD) You bloody old fool!
MRS. F-B	There has been an intruder. Somebody has plundered my privacy!
CATCHPOLE	Shall I telephone the Police, madam?
FRED	(quickly) I wouldn't do that, if I were you!
MRS. F-B	And why not?
FRED	By the time they get 'ere, it'll be too late.
MRS. F-B	Do you anticipate further carnage?
FRED	Oh, no! But the intruder will 'ave got away by then.
MRS. F-B	Then we must stalk him ourselves. Come along, Major!
CATCHPOLE	Yes, madam.
MRS. F-B	Mr. Baxter, Mr. Spook – you search out the back.
FRED	Eh? Oh – yes!
MRS. F-B	Mr. Mullins – you had better guard the front door in case he tries to make a break for it.
CHARLIE	What a good idea!
MRS. F-B	Major, I trust you have your pistol at the ready?
CATCHPOLE	Yes, madam. (He gets out his revolver again.)
MRS. F-B	If this is that escaped prisoner, he may be violent.
CATCHPOLE	(following her up the stairs) I doubt it, madam. According to the evening paper he was only inside for some quite trivial offence, and was going to be released a week on Friday! (He goes off after MRS. FLETCHER-BREWER.)
	(HAROLD and CHARLIE have gone very still. FRED, inwardly seething, turns and comes slowly to them.)
FRED	Everybody 'as their cross to bear, and I've got you two.
HAROLD	I told you I didn't know where the money was.

FRED	'Arold, do you see a smile on my lips?
HAROLD	No.
FRED	Do you see a friendly look in my eye?
HAROLD	No.
FRED	Do you sense a kind 'eart beating within my breast?
HAROLD	No-o!
FRED	That's because I am neither smiling nor friendly, and all that is in my 'eart at this moment is longing. Longing to reach out and take your 'ead in my 'ands – and crush it like a bloody walnut!
HAROLD	Oh, please don't do that!
FRED	Why not?
HAROLD	It'll remind me of Christmas.
	(FRED turns to CHARLIE, who smiles weakly.)
CHARLIE	I made a simple mistake.
FRED	(gently sarcastic) I wouldn't say that, Charlie. Out of all the men in that prison there was one we wanted. Just one – that's all. One bloke who could lead us all to a small fortune. And what do you do? Do you get that one bloke? Oh, no! Instead you spring darling 'Arold 'ere, who wouldn't 'ave the nerve to fiddle five bob from the 'ousekeeping money!
CHARLIE	(lamely) Well, they both had the same name.
FRED	So I suppose you thought it didn't matter which one you got?
CHARLIE	Well, I've never done this sort of thing before.
FRED	And you'll never do it again! (To HAROLD.) 'Adn't you got the bloody sense to tell 'im 'e'd made a mistake?
HAROLD	Aye – I did!
CHARLIE	Only after we got here.
FRED	And what was we supposed to do then? Take you back

	to the Governor and say, "We don't like the one we've got, can we change 'im for another?"
HAROLD	(smiling) Get away! They'd never 'ave done that.
FRED	(moving closer to HAROLD) Tell me, does your wife know where you are?
HAROLD	No. She thinks I'm still inside.
FRED	Then she'll 'ave a lovely surprise when she opens the evening paper, won't she?
HAROLD	(pleased) Aye. I've never 'ad me name in the paper before.
FRED	You'll be in it again soon.
HAROLD	Will I really?
FRED	When they fish you out of the river.
HAROLD	What river?
FRED	The river out 'ere! Because I tell you this, Spook, if you lead the Law to me that is where you will end up.
HAROLD	But I can't swim.
FRED	You won't need to. (He turns to CHARLIE.) Are you thinking 'ard?
CHARLIE	Oh, yes. Very.
FRED	'Ave you found a way out of our little dilemma?
CHARLIE	Yes.
FRED	Well?
CHARLIE	Run for it!
	(He starts to go, but FRED prevents him.)
FRED	Not without the money.
HAROLD	But we don't know where it is!
FRED	Then we'll 'ave to find out, won't we?
CHARLIE	We can't stay here. Suppose that girl suddenly remembers where she saw Harold?

FRED   Yes.   (To HAROLD.)   You would 'ave to go
            making fish eyes at 'er, wouldn't you?

HAROLD   I didn't make eyes at her!

FRED   You surprise me.

HAROLD   She just saw me, that's all.

FRED   And I suppose it was love at first sight?

HAROLD   No. She was visiting him.

FRED   Who?

HAROLD   The other one!

FRED   The other what?

HAROLD   Him!

CHARLIE   You don't mean — the other Spook?

HAROLD   Aye!

CHARLIE   The one I should have — ?

HAROLD   Aye!

CHARLIE   Oh, my God!

            (HAROLD stands alone, fearful. FRED turns to CHARLIE,
            his face brightening. He comes close to HAROLD, who
            cringes, expecting the worst.)

FRED   'Arold — do you notice anything different about me?

            (HAROLD looks slowly at FRED, and is rather surprised
            at what he sees.)

HAROLD   Yes. You're smiling!

FRED   Yes. I am smiling, and the 'atred in my 'eart 'as
            lifted.

HAROLD   Has it? Oh, good!

FRED   Charlie boy, this is just what we needed.

CHARLIE   Oh? Is it?

FRED   Why do you suppose that girl's 'ere?

CHARLIE   To have a quiet weekend with her father?

FRED	No! He's just a cover.
HAROLD	A cover?
FRED	To 'ide what she's really 'ere for.
HAROLD	And what's that?
FRED	To collect, of course!
CHARLIE	Collect?
FRED	The money the other Spook left 'ere!
CHARLIE	Yes, of course!
FRED	So all we 'ave to do now is wait till she gets the stuff from where it's 'idden – then grab 'er, take the money and scarper!
HAROLD	All of it?
FRED	Why not?
HAROLD	It's not ours.
FRED	(in despair) Why did I 'ave to get lumbered with you? Now listen – this is what we do. Charlie – you and me 'll keep a look-out upstairs – right?
CHARLIE	Er – right!
FRED	'Arold – you'll be sleeping down 'ere.
HAROLD	Nay, I'm up there in Willow.
FRED	Not any more. You're down 'ere on that.
HAROLD	On the sofa?
FRED	Yes.
HAROLD	All night?
FRED	Yes.
HAROLD	Oh. Well, we'll keep each other warm, anyhow.
FRED	What are you talking about?
HAROLD	That girl's sleeping down here, too.
CHARLIE	(shaking his head sadly) No, Harold.

HAROLD	No?
CHARLIE	No. She's going to be in <u>your</u> room.
HAROLD	(put out) Oh - why?
FRED	Because you've got to be down 'ere, 'aven't you? Down 'ere with your eyes open!
	(EDNA comes in D.L. with a pillow and a pillow case. She crosses to the sofa.)
EDNA	I ought to 'ave overtime, that's what. One of these days I'll write to the Queen. See what 'Er Majesty 'as to say about it. (She continues with the bed-making.) Working, working - all hours of the day and night. This isn't what Mrs. Pankhurst chained 'erself up for -
	(CATCHPOLE, still carrying his revolver, comes downstairs.)
CATCHPOLE	No sign of an intruder up there.
CHARLIE	No, of course not.
CATCHPOLE	Did you have a look out the back?
FRED	Eh? Oh, yes! Even the pigs are sleeping.
CHARLIE	I expect she imagined the whole thing. Been watching too much television.
	(POLLY and MR. PARKINSON wander in D.L.)
CATCHPOLE	I trust the cook managed to find you some food, miss.
POLLY	Oh, yes, thank you.
MR. P.	Is that all we're going to get?
POLLY	Dad! (To CATCHPOLE.) It was very nice, thank you.
MR. P.	Bit of cold spam and some yellow lettuce.
POLLY	(quietly to him) Will you be quiet?
MR. P.	I'd have been better off at home with a cold pie in front of the telly.

POLLY   Don't take any notice of him.   (To MR.
             PARKINSON.)   Silly old fool.

             (MR. PARKINSON, muttering to himself, settles in the
             armchair D.L.)

CATCHPOLE   I hope you'll be comfortable down here, miss. Not
             exactly the penthouse at the Dorchester.

POLLY   I'll be all right.

FRED   Oh - er - as a matter of fact, we were just discussing
             that. Weren't we, 'Arold?

HAROLD   Were we?

FRED   And we decided we couldn't let a young lady spend the
             night on the sofa. Didn't we, 'Arold?

HAROLD   Did we?

CATCHPOLE   I'm afraid there's no alternative. All the rooms is
             'eavily booked.

CHARLIE   Ah, yes - but, you see, Harold wants her to sleep in his
             room.

             (POLLY and CATCHPOLE react.)

POLLY   (coldly)   I'd sooner sleep on the sofa, if it's all the
             same to you!

CHARLIE   Oh, Harold won't be in the room! No, no. He wants
             to give up his room to you. Don't you, Harold?

HAROLD   'Aven't much choice, 'ave I?

POLLY   Oh, you don't have to bother. I'll be all right down
             here, really.

HAROLD   That's all right, then. I'll go up to bed -

             (He starts but FRED has a restraining hold on him.)

             No?

FRED   No, 'Arold.

CHARLIE   (to POLLY)   We insist.

CATCHPOLE   I think you should accept the offer, miss.

POLLY	(rather reluctant) Oh. All right, then. Thanks.
EDNA	So I take it you won't be wanting the bed on the sofa?
POLLY	No, thanks.
EDNA	(long-suffering) Right. (She starts to collect up the bedclothes.)
POLLY	(to HAROLD) You know, I must try to think where it was I saw you.
HAROLD	I wouldn't try too hard, if I were you.
	(EDNA makes for the door D.L., with the blankets.)
CATCHPOLE	Edna! Where you going?
EDNA	To put the blankets away.
CATCHPOLE	And where do you suppose Mr. Spook is going to sleep?
EDNA	I don't know!
CATCHPOLE	On the sofa, Edna. On the sofa.
EDNA	I see. (She sighs deeply, crosses back to the sofa and starts again to make up the bed.)
CATCHPOLE	Of course, I believe there is a spare bed in your room, Mr. Mullins.
CHARLIE	Oh. Yes. That's right. I've got my case on it.
CATCHPOLE	Well, perhaps you wouldn't mind sharing?
CHARLIE	(turning delightedly to POLLY) Well, I don't know how the young lady feels –
CATCHPOLE	I was thinking of Mr. Spook.
CHARLIE	Oh, were you?
CATCHPOLE	Perhaps Mr. Spook could have your spare bed.
CHARLIE	(without enthusiasm) Yes. I suppose he could.
EDNA	I see. (She dumps the bedclothes in an untidy heap and makes for the stairs, thoroughly put out.) I wish you'd make up your bleedin' minds!
CATCHPOLE	Edna!

EDNA   One of these days I'll go on strike, that's what I'll do, go on strike!

CATCHPOLE   Edna!

EDNA   (halfway up the stairs)   Well?

CATCHPOLE   Remember what I pay you for.

EDNA   You 'aven't! Not for three weeks! So call to your 'eart's content, because I'm going to bed!

CATCHPOLE   Then on your way you can show Mr. Parkinson and his daughter to their rooms, can't you?

POLLY   Yes. Come on, Dad. You can't go to sleep there.

MR. P.   (waking from a doze)   Eh? What-you-say?

POLLY   (helping him to his feet)   You'll have to go to your room.

MR. P.   I'm not sleeping in no box-room. I'd sooner sleep down here -

POLLY   Oh, all right. Look - I'll sleep in the box-room. Okay? You can sleep in my room.

MR. P.   I didn't know you'd got a room.

POLLY   Yes, I have - now.   (To HAROLD.)   What's the name of it, love?

HAROLD   I'm not 'aving 'im in there -

FRED   'Arold!

HAROLD   I don't mind her - but not 'im!

FRED   (firm)   Spook!   (Turning to POLLY with a smile.)   It's Willow, miss.

POLLY   Oh, thanks. All right, Dad? You'll be in Willow instead.

MR. P.   (as they go towards the stairs)   It's not another box-room, is it?

EDNA   (who has been waiting impatiently)   Are you coming or not?

MR. P.	You don't have to shout, you know.
	(He and POLLY go off upstairs, followed by an irate EDNA. CATCHPOLE starts to tidy up the blankets.)
CATCHPOLE	Well, you won't be needing these now, Mr. Spook.
	(FRED and CHARLIE exchange a quick look, and then move down to CATCHPOLE.)
CHARLIE	Oh - er - actually - I think he really ought to sleep down here.
CATCHPOLE	But the spare bed, Mr. Mullins - ?
CHARLIE	It's far too comfortable for him.
FRED	Yes. It's not what he's used to.
CHARLIE	He wouldn't sleep a wink. He'll be much better down here. Won't you, Harold?
HAROLD	No!
CHARLIE	There you are, you see! So that's all fixed.
CATCHPOLE	(doubtfully) Very well, Mr. Mullins, if you say so. But I hope he won't be too cold down here. Gets awfully chilly in the night.
CHARLIE	You'll wrap up well, won't you, Harold?
HAROLD	Oh, 'eck!
	(MRS. FLETCHER-BREWER comes abruptly down the stairs.)
MRS. F-B	(imperiously) Well? Where are they?
CHARLIE	They've just gone to bed.
MRS. F-B	What?
CHARLIE	Well, it's very late.
MRS. F-B	What are you talking about?
CHARLIE	I don't know. What are you talking about?
MRS. F-B	The Police! The Police!
FRED	(alarmed) Where?

MRS. F–B	They don't seem to be here!
FRED	Thank God for that.
MRS. F–B	And why not? Tell me that! Major, you were descending to summon them.
CATCHPOLE	Was I?
MRS. F–B	You went down the stairs shouting, "Reinforcements!"
CHARLIE	(to CATCHPOLE, amused) You didn't, did you?
CATCHPOLE	Ah, yes. But, you see, there was people down here. I had to deal with them first.
MRS. F–B	And all the time, Major, the grass has been growing!
CHARLIE	Yes. It's quite long outside.
MRS. F–B	Then do it now, Major! Do it now!
CHARLIE	What? Cut the grass?
MRS. F–B	Call the Police!
CATCHPOLE	Yes, madam. (He starts to go towards the telephone.)
FRED	I wouldn't do that!
CATCHPOLE	Why not?
FRED	Well, we don't know for certain there has been an intruder.
MRS. F–B	You have my evidence!
CHARLIE	You call that evidence? A few pairs of rumpled knickers. Anyway, the poor old policeman's probably in bed by now.
MRS. F–B	At this time of night?
CHARLIE	Can you imagine how you'd feel if you were dragged out of bed in the middle of the night and made to fight your way into a pair of boots?
MRS. F–B	It is not the middle of the night.
CHARLIE	It jolly soon will be!
FRED	Besides, you might be calling 'im out 'ere on a wild

	goose chase.
MRS. F-B	I have the evidence of my eyes! Catchpole - the tele-phone!
CATCHPOLE	Yes, madam.
	(He makes for the telephone again, but again they restrain him.)
CHARLIE	Suppose you do send for the Police? The poor old constable's going to have to push his wife out of bed, get himself dressed, put on his boots -
HAROLD	Let the cat out.
CHARLIE	(after a glance at HAROLD) Let the cat out, push his wife back in bed again, go out the front door -
HAROLD	Trip over the cat.
CHARLIE	(another glance at HAROLD) Trip over the cat, get on his bike and pedal like mad all the way here. Can you imagine the state he'll be in when he arrives, all puffing and blowing on the doorstep?
FRED	He'll be in no mood for funny stories, I can tell you. The Police don't like being messed about, y'know.
MRS. F-B	I demand - !
CHARLIE	Much better wait until the morning. After all, if there was an intruder in your bedroom he's not going to intrude again, is he?
HAROLD	Not likely!
FRED	And if he did come back - well, there are plenty of us to deal with 'im. Four able-bodied men!
CATCHPOLE	(weakening) Yes - and I've got my old Service revolver!
CHARLIE	And I've got my old suspenders.
MRS. F-B	(reluctantly) Very well. But, I warn you, if any-thing untoward occurs - I hold you all responsible! And of one thing you may be certain - I shall be locking my bedroom door!

CHARLIE   Oh, what a pity.

                (CAROL comes quickly down the stairs, in a high state
                of distress.)

CAROL   Major Catchpole! Major Catchpole!

CATCHPOLE   What is it?

CAROL   Outside – quick! There's something moving in the
                garden!

CATCHPOLE   Oh, lord! Those bloody pigs are out again!   (He
                goes racing out of the front door, leaving it wide open.)

                (As CATCHPOLE is going out of the door, POLLY runs on
                urgently from upstairs, pointing excitedly at HAROLD.)

POLLY   Here! I've just remembered where I saw you!

CHARLIE)
FRED   )   (together)   Harold!

HAROLD   Ooh!

                (HAROLD, panic-stricken, races to seek shelter in the
                cupboard and pulls open the door. NORAH is there.
                She beams delightedly.)

NORAH   I thought you were never coming!

                (She grabs him, and is trying to pull him, protesting,
                into the cupboard with CHARLIE and FRED rushing to his
                aid as –

                THE CURTAIN FALLS

ACT THREE

The early hours of the next morning. The stage is lit
only by a dim red glow from the dying fire and the moonlight coming through the window.

HAROLD is sitting on the sofa. He has a blanket around
his shoulders and is the picture of dejection. He looks
quickly towards the stairs as he hears a step on the landing. He rises and hides at the L. end of the sofa. A
figure comes into view in the shadows at the top of the
stairs and creeps quietly down. It moves below the sofa
towards the fireplace. HAROLD leaps out from cover
and drags the protesting figure to the ground, where a
small struggle ensues.

CHARLIE   Get off, you bloody fool! It's only me!

               (HAROLD gets to his feet, followed by a rumpled
               CHARLIE.)

               What do you think you're doing?

HAROLD   I thought you were the girl.

CHARLIE   Couldn't you tell the difference?

HAROLD   You shouldn't 'ave come creeping down the stairs like
               that.

CHARLIE   I wanted to make sure you hadn't dozed off.

HAROLD   (pulling the blanket around himself again)   I'm too
               cold to doze off. Oh, I do wish I was nicely tucked up
               in my cell.

CHARLIE   Cheer up. You'll soon be back in again. You'll
               probably get about fifty years after this.   (He hears
               a noise.)   S'sh! Someone coming.

               (They hide quickly behind the sofa. CAROL, in
               dressing-gown and slippers, comes down the stairs. She
               turns on the lights and crosses to the sofa, looking for
               something. Not finding it there, she goes off D.L. The
               heads of CHARLIE and HAROLD appear slowly over the

back of the sofa, turn and look at each other and then duck down out of sight as CAROL returns. She crosses below the sofa to D.R. The heads appear again when she has passed the sofa and they watch her go off D.R.)

HAROLD   I'm going to sneeze.

CHARLIE   Be quiet!

HAROLD   But I can't 'elp it!

CHARLIE   S'sh!

(HAROLD sneezes loudly, and CHARLIE pulls him down behind the sofa as CAROL returns with her handbag. She stops in the doorway, obviously having heard the sneeze.)

CAROL   Who's there?

(She shrugs and moves towards the stairs. As she does so, HAROLD and CHARLIE, on their hands and knees, creep around the L. end of the sofa to below it to avoid being seen as she goes upstage. HAROLD sneezes again. CHARLIE glares at him. CAROL stops, turns and starts to come downstage again. As she does so, they reverse the previous move and creep back to behind the sofa.)

Is anybody there?

(After a moment, she gives up again and moves up towards the stairs. Again the boys crawl round the L. end of the sofa to below it. HAROLD is about to sneeze again. CHARLIE tries to stop him, but it is no good and he sneezes loudly. CAROL stops and comes quickly downstage to R. of the sofa. HAROLD escapes to behind the sofa, but she is too quick for CHARLIE and catches him on all fours below the sofa.)

What on earth are you doing?

CHARLIE   Sneezing.

CAROL   Yes. I heard you.

CHARLIE   It's those pigs. I always sneeze when there are pigs about.

CAROL	But the pigs are outside.
CHARLIE	Yes – they are now. But when I came down they were in here.
CAROL	In here?
CHARLIE	Yes. I chased them out. But when I got back I started sneezing.
CAROL	Why didn't you turn the lights on?
CHARLIE	I always sneeze in the dark.
	(HAROLD sneezes again. CAROL looks quickly at CHARLIE, who pretends it was him.)
	I beg your pardon. There I go again!
CAROL	For a moment I thought you were that escaped prisoner.
CHARLIE	Oh, I don't think he's anywhere around here.
	(HAROLD sneezes. CHARLIE again reacts as if it was him.)
	I'm so sorry. I really will have to wrap myself up a bit. (He puts the blanket around his shoulders.)
CAROL	Let me help you. (She goes to assist him with his blanket.)
CHARLIE	Oh, thank you. (He settles himself comfortably, and in the process takes her hand.)
CAROL	Mr. Mullins –
CHARLIE	H'm?
CAROL	You're holding my hand.
CHARLIE	Oh, yes. So I am. I thought there was something. Do you want it back?
CAROL	Yes, please.
CHARLIE	Right, then. (He releases her hand, but they have both quite enjoyed it.)
	(From upstairs voices are heard.)
FRED	(off) I'm sure you must 'ave been mistaken.

MRS. F—B   (off)   I tell you, I distinctly heard voices!

CAROL   It's Mummy!

CHARLIE   Well, now you'll have to marry me.

(MRS. FLETCHER—BREWER, in nightdress, dressing—gown and slippers, appears at the top of the stairs with FRED. He is also in pyjamas and dressing—gown.)

MRS. F—B   Carol! Mr. Mullins! What are you two doing out of bed?

CHARLIE   What were you two doing <u>in</u> bed?

MRS.F—B   I heard voices and fearing the worst I summoned Mr. Baxter from his room.

CHARLIE   And that <u>was</u> the worst.

MRS. F—B   What is the meaning of this midnight rendezvous?

CAROL   I came down to look for my handbag.

CHARLIE   And I was helping her.

MRS. F—B   You just happened to be down here?

CHARLIE   Yes. You happened to be up there, and I happened to be down here.

(A loud sneeze from HAROLD behind the sofa. CHARLIE turns at once to MRS. FLETCHER—BREWER.)

Bless you!

MRS. F—B   I beg your pardon?

CHARLIE   That's quite all right. Here — we mustn't let you catch cold, must we?   (He takes off his blanket and drapes it around her shoulders.)

MRS. F—B   Take your blanket off me! I am not a loose horse!

CHARLIE   Oh. My mistake.   (He takes the blanket back again.)

MRS. F—B   Mr. Mullins, I am looking for an explanation.

CHARLIE   You won't find one here.

CAROL   Mummy, there's nothing to explain —

MRS. F—B	It is coincidence, then, that I find you down here – alone with a man and scantily clad?
CHARLIE	I'm not scantily clad. I'm fully–dressed plus. (He indicates his blanket.)
MRS. F—B	When I was a girl I'd never trust a man who carried a blanket.
CAROL	Mr. Mullins was seeing to the pigs.
MRS. F—B	He didn't appear to be seeing to the pigs when I came in. He was on the sofa.
CAROL	He'd finished, then. He was resting.
MRS. F—B	(the voice of thunder) Resting?
CHARLIE	So would you be if you'd chased a couple of pigs around the place.
MRS. F—B	I would never choose to chase a pig!
CHARLIE	No. I bet you wouldn't even chase a pork sausage.

(HAROLD sneezes. It is obvious to all that the sound came from behind the sofa. MRS. FLETCHER–BREWER crosses to above it as HAROLD creeps out on all fours and makes for the door D.L.)

MRS. F—B	Mr. Spook!

(HAROLD stops in his tracks and turns to look at them.)

HAROLD	'Ullo.
FRED	You bloody old fool!
MRS. F—B	Mr. Baxter, kindly moderate your language! I would be obliged if you would persuade your friends to retire for the night. Come, Carol! (To FRED.) There are some of us who need our beauty sleep!
FRED	(quietly) Yes – some more than others.

(MRS. FLETCHER–BREWER sweeps off with CAROL, somewhat reluctantly, in her wake. FRED moves to between CHARLIE and HAROLD, who has now risen. He puts his face very near to HAROLD's and speaks as to a child.)

	Spook. Up there by the front door there's a great big bell.
HAROLD	Is there?
FRED	It's a fire alarm bell.
HAROLD	(impressed) Is it?
FRED	Do you know what I'd do if I were you?
HAROLD	No.
FRED	I'd go up there and I'd fetch that bell. And I'd bring it down to the middle of the room – and I'd ring it for all I was worth!
HAROLD	What for?
FRED	Then you'd be sure of waking up the rest of the bleedin' 'ouse! (He turns to CHARLIE.) And what about you?
CHARLIE	Me?
FRED	You're supposed to be standing by for the big moment, not sitting down 'ere snoggin' on the sofa!
CHARLIE	I was doing no such thing.
FRED	No?
CHARLIE	I wish I had been.
FRED	Could it be that you two are not dedicated to the task in 'and? We are supposed to be lying in wait, making ourselves as inconspicuous as possible – not stampeding about the place like a 'erd of bloody buffalo!
CHARLIE	It wasn't our fault the girl came down to get her handbag.
FRED	Couldn't you have 'idden yourselves until she'd gone?
CHARLIE	It was just one of those things that happen.
FRED	That's what your mother must 'ave said when your father came in and saw you for the first time! Do you suppose we 'ave now managed to lull the girl Polly into a sense of security, or 'ave we made such a bleedin' racket that she 'as now abandoned the idea of collecting the stuff?

CHARLIE	I should think she's given up.
HAROLD	Aye! We may as well go 'ome.
	(He and CHARLIE start to go.)
FRED	Come back 'ere!
	(HAROLD and CHARLIE walk back again.)
HAROLD	Oh. I thought we were off.
FRED	We're not going 'ome, 'Arold. We're going to try again.
HAROLD	Oh, 'eck.
FRED	All right, Charlie. Let's 'ave the lights off, for a start, shall we?
	(CHARLIE goes to the stairs and turns off the lights. He hears something and comes back to them quickly.)
CHARLIE	There's somebody coming!
FRED	Down 'ere, quick!
	(They hide up near the cupboard where there is plenty of shadow. NORAH, in nightdress, dressing-gown, slippers and curlers, comes down the stairs cautiously.)
CHARLIE	(in a whisper) It's Mrs. Catchpole!
HAROLD	(in a whisper) Oh, 'eck.
CHARLIE	(in a whisper) Do you think she's sleep-walking?
FRED	(in a whisper) No. She always looks like that.
	(NORAH crosses below them to the bar, opens the register and, with the aid of a small torch, starts to look at it.)
HAROLD	(in a whisper) What's she doing?
FRED	(in a whisper) Looking at the register.
HAROLD	(in a whisper) What for?
FRED	(in a whisper) I expect she's forgotten which room you're in.
	(HAROLD reacts in horror and knocks something over.)

NORAH turns quickly to see three shadowy figures in the gloom. She screams and falls in a dead faint.)

Now see what you've done! You'll 'ave everybody down now bar the marines!

CHARLIE   We'd better pick her up.

FRED   All right - quick!

(They go to her.)

I'll take the top end.

CHARLIE   And I'll take the heavy end.

FRED   Come on, Spook! Don't just stand there!

(With difficulty they pick up NORAH, and put her on the sofa.)

FRED   Blimey! Just look at 'er.

HAROLD   Reminds me of a nightmare I once 'ad.

(The lights go on on the landing.)

FRED   Quick - someone coming!

(He makes for the cupboard, taking HAROLD with him. CHARLIE takes a flower out of a vase and lays it reverently on NORAH's chest. He then follows the others out into the cupboard and shuts the door. MRS. FLETCHER-BREWER appears at the top of the stairs and peers down into the darkness below.)

MRS. F-B   Who is that down there screaming?   (She turns on the lights, comes down to the sofa and sees NORAH lying there.)   Mrs. Catchpole! What a dreadful sight!   (For a second she is undecided, then her eyes light on the alarm bell. She goes quickly to get it and starts to ring it loudly. She goes up the stairs, ringing the bell and calling out.)   Major Catchpole! Quickly! Send for the Police! Major Catchpole! Everybody out of your beds!   (She disappears from view and continues to ring and call offstage.)

(The men come out of the cupboard.)

FRED	Come on - give me a 'and!
CHARLIE	What are we going to do?
FRED	If we leave 'er lying here they'll call the Police. Let's put 'er in the cupboard till she comes round.
	(They pick up NORAH again and carry her off into the cupboard, closing the door behind them. MRS. FLETCHER-BREWER returns, still carrying the bell, followed by CATCHPOLE, in his pyjamas and bare feet, and CAROL, hastily pulling on a dressing-gown.)
MRS. F-B	There was a scream, so I came downstairs, and there she was - lying on the sofa!
	(They all stop on arrival at the sofa, where there is no sign of NORAH.)
CATCHPOLE	Doesn't appear to be there now, madam.
MRS. F-B	She was lying flat! With a flower on her bosom!
CATCHPOLE	Not like her.
MRS. F-B	So I rang this thing! (She starts to ring the bell again.)
CATCHPOLE	Madam - madam, please - (He attempts to restrain her.) - if you could only stop ringing the bell!
	(She stops.)
	Thank you, madam.
MRS. F-B	Do you think I would drag you out of your bed under false pretences?
CATCHPOLE	No, of course not. But, as you see, the sofa is uninhabited.
MRS. F-B	Carol, you will bear me out. There was a scream.
CAROL	Yes. I heard a scream.
CATCHPOLE	But did you see my wife?
CAROL	Well, no - I didn't.
MRS. F-B	Major, you do not seem unduly perturbed by the possibility that all is not well with your wife. Didn't

	you hear her leave your room?
CATCHPOLE	Yes, madam. But that was hardly sufficient reason for raisin' the alarm.
MRS. F-B	Didn't you wonder where she was going?
CATCHPOLE	I assumed there was a perfectly simple explanation.
CAROL	Don't you think we ought to have a look for her?
CATCHPOLE	A good idea, miss. No doubt she's in the kitchen. This way, ladies – follow me!

(As they make for the door D.L., MRS. FLETCHER-BREWER picks up the poker from near the fireplace.)

| MRS. F-B | Under the circumstances I think it would be best for us to be armed!   (She follows the others off D.L.) |

(The boys come out of the cupboard, carrying NORAH between them.)

| FRED | Get 'er on the sofa, quick! I think she's coming round. |

(They get her to the sofa and sit her down. FRED and HAROLD sit either side to hold her up. CHARLIE stands behind. They pat her hands, wave a handkerchief in front of her face, etc., in an attempt to revive her. She stirs, opens her eyes and sees HAROLD.)

NORAH	Ah! You've come for me at last! (She embraces him heartily.)
HAROLD	'Ere – get 'er off!
FRED	(attempting to disentangle them) Now, now – just a minute – !

(She turns, sees FRED and promptly faints again into HAROLD's lap.)

CHARLIE	Now see what you've done!
FRED	I didn't know she was going to faint again, did I?
CHARLIE	What do you expect? Sitting about in your pyjamas. It's enough to make anybody faint.
FRED	We'll 'ave to get 'er back to 'er room.

CHARLIE	(doubtfully) It's a long way.
FRED	Look, Charlie boy, as long as people go on chasing in and out of 'ere like this, we've got no chance of getting that money, 'ave we?
CHARLIE	Well, I'm not carrying her all the way up there.
HAROLD	I wish somebody would get 'er off my knee.
FRED	We'll 'ave to bring 'er round.
CHARLIE	Here, let me do it. We don't want her seeing you again.
	(He changes places with FRED, pulls NORAH upright, pats her face, etc.)
FRED	The only way to get 'er back to 'er room is to give 'er an incentive.
HAROLD	What's that?
FRED	Sort of a bait. You know – like cheese in a mousetrap.
HAROLD	(unsuspecting) And what are we going to use for the cheese?
	(FRED and CHARLIE both turn to look at HAROLD, smiling broadly. He reacts.)
HAROLD	Oh, no! Not me! No!
FRED	You'll only be the carrot dangling in front of the donkey!
HAROLD	Aye, but will the donkey catch up with the carrot?
FRED	That depends how fast you can run.
CHARLIE	She's coming round!
FRED	Harold – up the stairs, quick!
HAROLD	No – I won't!
CHARLIE	You can keep a few paces ahead of her.
HAROLD	No!
FRED	Spook –
HAROLD	Oh, 'eck. (Reluctantly he goes to a position at the

foot of the stairs.)

NORAH	(coming to) Oh, it's you, Mr. Mullins. What must you think of me?
CHARLIE	Don't you worry. You'll be all right again after a good night's rest.
NORAH	I don't know what came over me.
CHARLIE	Look - er - there's Harold.
NORAH	What?
CHARLIE	(confidentially) Harold. (He jerks his head towards the stairs.)

(She turns and sees HAROLD. He smiles a sickly smile.)

NORAH	Ooh. Doesn't he look sweet?
FRED	(quietly) Oh, blimey!
CHARLIE	He'll take you back to your room.
NORAH	(surprised and delighted) He will?
CHARLIE	Yes.
NORAH	Oooooh!

(She gets up enthusiastically and goes quickly towards HAROLD. He sees her coming and starts off up the stairs.)

Harold - wait for me!

(She races after him up the stairs. CHARLIE and FRED shake hands as MRS. FLETCHER-BREWER, CAROL and CATCHPOLE return from D.L.)

CHARLIE	There you are, Fred! I told you I heard someone ringing a bell.
MRS. F-B	It was me! (She rings the bell.)
CATCHPOLE	(restraining her) Madam - please - allow me - (He takes the bell from her and puts it down on the mantelpiece.)
MRS. F-B	Did you see her?

CHARLIE	Who?
MRS. F-B	Mrs. Catchpole! She was lying on the sofa.
CHARLIE	What on earth for?
MRS. F-B	She had passed out.
CHARLIE	You mean she'd been drinking?
CATCHPOLE	My wife may have her faults, but alcohol ain't on her list.
CAROL	There was a scream.
MRS. F-B	And I came downstairs.
CHARLIE	Perhaps that's why she screamed.
MRS. F-B	The scream came first!
FRED	There was nobody on the sofa when we came down, was there, Charlie?
MRS. F-B	I saw her with my own eyes.
CHARLIE	(to CAROL) Did you see her, too?
CAROL	No. I was upstairs.
CHARLIE	(turning to MRS. FLETCHER-BREWER) So we've only your word for it, then?
MRS. F-B	What are you getting at?
CHARLIE	What did you have for dinner?
MRS. F-B	What's that got to do with it?
FRED	Something might 'ave disagreed with you.
CHARLIE	Onion soup, for instance! Have you ever disagreed with onion soup?
MRS. F-B	You're wasting time!
CHARLIE	Yes, I know - I mean - for all we know she's still upstairs.
CATCHPOLE	I'll go and see if she's back in her room. (He goes towards the stairs.)
CHARLIE	(aside) Yes. She should be there by now.

MRS. F-B	I will accompany you, Major. Come, Carol! (With a look at CHARLIE.) There is more to this than meets the eye!
	(She follows CATCHPOLE off upstairs, with CAROL behind her.)
CHARLIE	I hope Harold's got her back all right.
FRED	He's 'ad plenty of time. I'm getting worried.
CHARLIE	About Harold?
FRED	No! About the money! That girl's 'ardly likely to risk getting it now - not with all this circus going on.
CHARLIE	I suppose we'd better forget all about it, then.
FRED	I'm not leaving 'ere without that money - not even if I 'ave to pull the place to pieces brick by brick!
	(From upstairs a loud banging on a door, and CATCH-POLE's voice calling out.)
	Now what the 'ell's 'appened?
	(CAROL runs on.)
CAROL	It's Mrs. Catchpole!
CHARLIE	What's happened to her?
CAROL	She's in her bedroom!
FRED	There you are - what did I tell you?
CAROL	But the door's locked - and there's a man inside!
CHARLIE	Is she shouting for help?
CAROL	No, but -
CHARLIE	Then there's nothing to worry about.
CAROL	Will you please come and help break the door down? (She runs off again.)
FRED	That bloody fool Spook! What's he doing in there?
CHARLIE	I expect she caught him up and dragged him in.
FRED	Well, now he's got in he'll 'ave to get out!

CHARLIE	There's only one way he can do that.
FRED	How?
CHARLIE	Our old friend the ivy!
	(They race out of the front door. The moment they have gone, POLLY and MR. PARKINSON come downstairs. She is in pyjamas, dressing-gown and slippers; he in a raincoat over his pyjamas.)
MR. P.	Is it time to get up already? I've only just gone to bed.
POLLY	No, Dad. I told you. I heard the fire bell.
MR. P.	What do I want a walk for at this time of night?
POLLY	No, Dad! There must be a fire.
MR. P.	There's a fire over there.
POLLY	They were ringing the bell.
MR. P.	What-you-say?
POLLY	The fire bell!
MR. P.	(looking towards the fireplace) It's nearly out. No point in ringing a bell.
	(A cry from outside as HAROLD falls from the ivy.)
POLLY	Did you hear that?
MR. P.	What-you-say?
POLLY	Must be the fire brigade.
MR. P.	What they want the fire brigade for? If I spat on that I'd put it out. (He wanders towards the door D.L.)
POLLY	Where you going, Dad?
MR. P.	I'm a bit peckish. Wonder if they've got some food out here - (He wanders out D.L.)
	(The front door opens and CHARLIE comes in, looking to see if the coast is clear. He sees POLLY.)
POLLY	Is it out there?
CHARLIE	It is at the moment. But we're bringing it in.

POLLY	Isn't there any danger?
CHARLIE	Not if we get it in quick enough.
POLLY	But you got it out all right?
CHARLIE	Oh, yes. We got it out. It's getting it back in that's the trouble.
POLLY	What do you mean?
CHARLIE	I dunno. What do _you_ mean?
POLLY	I'm talking about the fire.
CHARLIE	Oh, that! Yes, that's out long ago. That's why it's so chilly in here.
	(MRS. FLETCHER-BREWER storms in at the top of the stairs.)
MRS. F-B	Mr. Mullins!
CHARLIE	(with a broad smile) Still running about?
MRS. F-B	So _that's_ why you couldn't! I wondered why and now I know.
CHARLIE	Well, that's more than I do.
MRS. F-B	Why you didn't come to help the Major. He's been charging the bedroom door like an angry rhinoceros.
CHARLIE	Couldn't you have added your shoulder to his? I bet that would have done the trick.
MRS. F-B	I was waiting for you!
CHARLIE	And you'll have to wait a long time.
MRS. F-B	I might have known what you were up to. Down here dallying with another woman!
CHARLIE	And why not? I don't remember you proposing.
	(A shot from a revolver is heard upstairs.)
MRS. F-B	What was that?
CHARLIE	I think the Major's shot himself.
MRS. F-B	Come along! (She runs off again.)

(CHARLIE goes quickly to the front door.)

POLLY   Aren't you going to see what's happened?

CHARLIE   He's only trying to get into his wife's bedroom.
             (He goes out, closing the door behind him.)

             (POLLY realises her opportunity and goes quickly to the
             cupboard, opens the door, goes inside and closes it
             behind her. The front door opens and CHARLIE and
             FRED come in, half-supporting HAROLD.)

CHARLIE   You know, this is becoming a habit. If you're going to
             do this sort of thing much more we'll have to build a fire
             escape.

FRED   Spook, you ought to be ashamed – creeping into a lady's
             bedroom like that.

HAROLD   She caught up with me.

FRED   That wasn't the idea! You was supposed to be a carrot!

HAROLD   She dragged me in and locked the door.

CHARLIE   She'd need to.

HAROLD   The only way out was through the window.

CHARLIE   Lucky for you old Catchpole didn't catch you. He's
             very handy with that revolver of his.

             (Voices are heard on the landing.)

             Look out – he's coming! You'd better lie low for a
             while.   (He opens the cupboard door.)

HAROLD   Oh, no! Not that again!

CHARLIE   Nobody will bother you in there.

             (He pushes HAROLD inside and closes the door.
             CATCHPOLE comes downstairs, brandishing his revolver,
             followed by MRS. FLETCHER-BREWER and CAROL.)

CATCHPOLE   He got away!

CHARLIE   Is your wife very upset?

CATCHPOLE   She's having a lie down.

CHARLIE   It must have been quite a shock for her.

CATCHPOLE   Yes. I'm going to find him, and when I find him I'll kill him!

CHARLIE   There's no need for that, surely? After all, you've got your wife back. That's enough, isn't it?

FRED   (quietly)   I should think it's <u>more</u> than enough.

MRS. F–B   Well, Major? What about the next move?

CATCHPOLE   Yes. We must form a plan of action.

              (CATCHPOLE, MRS. FLETCHER–BREWER, FRED and CAROL go into a huddle L.C. and talk quietly. CHARLIE is about to join them when he hears a soft whistle from the stairs. NORAH tiptoes down a few steps and beckons to him. He glances quickly to make sure the others have not seen and goes to the foot of the stairs.)

NORAH   (in a whisper)   Is he all right?

CHARLIE   (in a whisper)   Harold? Oh, yes. I think so.

NORAH   (in a whisper)   Where is he?

CHARLIE   (in a whisper)   Oh – er – upstairs. In the linen cupboard.

NORAH   (in a whisper)   The little rascal!   (She goes off upstairs quickly.)

              (MRS. FLETCHER–BREWER emerges from the other group.)

MRS. F–B   Mr. Mullins! Come and join the party!

CHARLIE   Oh – yes – I'll bring a bottle of wine.

MRS. F–B   The search party!

CATCHPOLE   One thing is certain. The intruder must now be in the garden.

CHARLIE   That's what <u>you</u> think.

CATCHPOLE   What?

CHARLIE   I said that's what <u>I</u> think.

CATCHPOLE	We shall have to apprehend him.
MRS. F-B	And I shall call the Police.
FRED	(stopping her) Oh, no, you won't!
MRS. F-B	Do not obstruct my path!
CHARLIE	(quickly) They're already on their way.
FRED	(alarmed) What?
CHARLIE	Mr. Baxter telephoned them. Didn't you, Fred?
FRED	(relieved) Oh, yes – that's right. I did, didn't I?
CATCHPOLE	Come along, then – quick! He can't have gone far! (He runs out of the front door with his revolver at the high port.)
CHARLIE	(about to follow) Come on, Fred. Don't hang about.
FRED	I might get my pyjama bottoms wet. I'll go upstairs and keep a look-out there – in case he tries to get back inside again. (He goes towards the stairs.)
CHARLIE	But what about me?
FRED	That's all right. You've still got your shoes on. (He goes off upstairs.)
CHARLIE	Anything I can get you ladies?
MRS. F-B	Major Catchpole is in need of support!
CHARLIE	Oh, you've noticed that, too?
MRS. F-B	He's waiting for you outside! Are you a coward?
CHARLIE	How did you guess? (He goes out of the front door, closing it behind him.)
MRS. F-B	I should never have trusted that young man from the time he trespassed in my bay.

(The cupboard door bursts open and POLLY comes racing out. She is in rather a state and carries under her arm a small, dilapidated suitcase.)

What are you doing in that cupboard?

POLLY	There's a man in there!
MRS. F-B	That is no excuse!

(POLLY is already racing up the stairs.)

Where are you going?

(But POLLY disappears.)

Well, really!   (She makes for the cupboard.)
We'd better see who it is.

CAROL   (nervously)   Shouldn't we wait until the men come back?

MRS. F-B   And let the miscreant get away?   (She goes to the front door and gets a net from amongst her fishing tackle.)   Perhaps I shall land a fish to-day, after all! Come, Carol!   (She goes to the cupboard with her net at the ready.)

(CAROL joins her, rather tentatively.)

Whoever you are, come on out with your hands up!
(There is no response, so she looks inside.)   I don't think there's anybody there. The girl must be hysterical.

CAROL   I wonder what she was doing in there in the first place?

MRS. F-B   I shudder to think! Come - better make sure he isn't skulking in a corner. Is anybody there?

(They both disappear into the cupboard. EDNA, in dressing-gown, slippers and a bedcap, comes down the stairs, grumbling.)

EDNA   I don't know what's going on. Everybody shouting and ringing bells and firing guns. Anyone would think it was the Queen's birthday.

(She crosses upstage as MRS. FLETCHER-BREWER and CAROL re-appear from inside the cupboard. She screams with fright.)

MRS. F-B   Don't be ridiculous, Edna. It's only us.

EDNA   What were you doing coming out of that cupboard?

MRS. F-B   Having gone in, we had no alternative but to come out!

EDNA	A woman of your age ought to know better than to go wandering into strange cupboards like that.
MRS. F-B	Kindly remember your place!
EDNA	My place is in bed, that's where my place is. Not wandering about 'ere in the middle of the night.
MRS. F-B	This is an emergency! An escaped prisoner is at large.
EDNA	What am I supposed to do about it?
MRS. F-B	You can go and make us some tea. When this is over we shall be glad of it.
EDNA	No fear!
MRS. F-B	This is an emergency!
EDNA	I don't care if it's Mafeking night. Tea is what the cook makes.
MRS. F-B	But the cook is not here! The cook is at home!
EDNA	Very nice for the cook.
CAROL	Please, Edna. Just this once.
EDNA	(with a smile) Yes, miss, of course I will – (With a glare at MRS. FLETCHER-BREWER.) – now I've been asked! (She goes off D.L.)
MRS. F-B	It really is coming to something when one has to plead with the staff to perform their duties.

(The door behind the bar opens slowly. MRS. FLETCHER-BREWER and CAROL freeze. MR. PARKINSON comes out, eating some bread-and-cheese. He does not see them and goes to sit on the sofa. MRS. FLETCHER-BREWER gestures to CAROL to follow her, and they move down to behind the old man. She raises her net in readiness, and with a deft movement brings it down neatly over MR. PARKINSON's head.)

Got you! Now all I need is a gaff!

(The astonished old man looks about vaguely, the net over his face. The ladies move down to either side of him.)

MR. P.   What's going on?

MRS. F-B   You have come to the end of the road. The Police will
                be here at any moment.

MR. P.   It's only a bit of cheese. No harm in that, is there?

MRS. F-B   They will return you to the place from whence you came.

MR. P.   Do you think you could take this net off my head? I
                want to finish my cheese.

MRS. F-B   Carol, I think I saw some rope in the dining-room.

CAROL   Yes, Mummy.   (She goes out D.L.)

MR. P.   I suppose this is some sort of game? You young people
                are all the same. Always skylarking.   (He chuckles.)
                But I would like to finish my cheese.

                (CAROL returns with two pieces of cord.)

MRS. F-B   Ah, good!

CAROL   I suppose this is the man we're looking for?

MRS. F-B   Well, I've never seen him before. He's an intruder all
                right. You only have to look at his face. Here - you
                take this.

                (She gives the net to CAROL, who puts it down against
                the wall.)

                Now - stand up, you - and no tricks!

MR. P.   What-you-say?

MRS. F-B   Stand up! Stand up!

                (Bewildered, MR. PARKINSON stands up and permits
                his hands and feet to be tied.)

                Right - sit down!

MR. P.   (sitting)   I don't understand -

MRS. F-B   There! He won't get away in a hurry.

MR. P.   Now I can't eat my cheese.

MRS. F-B   Come, Carol! Let's go and break the good news to the
                Major.

(They go out of the front door. EDNA comes on D.L.
with a tray of tea things. She puts it down on the table
in front of the sofa. She is about to go when she notices
MR. PARKINSON tied up on the sofa.)

EDNA

Oh, you're 'ere, are you? I suppose you'll want some
tea, too? Now I'll 'ave to get another cup.   (She
crosses to D.L., then stops and turns.)   Here - what
you all tied up for? This is no time for being tied up.
There's an emergency on. Didn't you know? Just a
minute - I'll get some scissors.

(She crosses upstage, and as she does so HAROLD comes
out of the cupboard. She screams and faints into his
arms. He is uncertain what to do with her for a moment,
then puts her in the cupboard and closes the door. He
breathes a sigh of relief and makes for the stairs but
NORAH appears at the top of them.)

NORAH

Naughty! Naughty! You weren't in the cupboard,
were you?

HAROLD

No. I was in the wine cellar.

NORAH

Never mind. I've found you now.

(She starts down the stairs quickly. HAROLD panics,
turns and runs out D.L. with NORAH, beaming joyfully,
in hot pursuit. The moment they have gone, POLLY
comes downstairs.)

POLLY

Dad! Dad, where are you?   (She sees him.)
I'd better get you back to your room.   (She arrives
at the sofa and sees his predicament.)   Whatever
'appened to you?

MR. P.

I went to get some bread-and-cheese.

POLLY

But you're all tied up!

MR. P.

I think it's some sort of game.

POLLY

Game? Funny sort of game. Come on, let's get you out
of this.   (Untying his cords.)   You see what
'appens to you the moment I let you out of my sight.

MR. P.

You missed the best part.

POLLY	Oh? And what was that?
MR. P.	(quite pleased) I had a net over my face. (He smiles happily.)
POLLY	Come on, Dad. It'll be time to get up soon. (She leads him towards the stairs.)
MR. P.	Bedtime already? I've only just got up.
POLLY	Oh, come on!
MR. P.	(as they go) One thing you can say about this place. It's very lively.
POLLY	Lively? I feel half-dead.
MR. P.	Well, what do you expect? I'm an old man.
	(They disappear up the stairs. The front door opens and MRS. FLETCHER-BREWER, CATCHPOLE, CHARLIE and CAROL come in quickly.)
MRS. F-B	What you men would do without us women I shudder to think. While you were running about in the garden, we have overpowered the intruder!
	(They arrive at the sofa and look at it. CHARLIE and CATCHPOLE exchange a look.)
CHARLIE	I don't see anybody. Do you, Major?
CATCHPOLE	Nobody.
MRS. F-B	He was there – on the sofa!
CHARLIE	You'll have to have yourself seen to, y'know.
MRS. F-B	I beg your pardon?
CHARLIE	You can't go on like this. Imagining people on sofas all the time.
MRS. F-B	We tied him up and put him on the sofa! Didn't we, Carol?
CAROL	Yes, of course we did.
CATCHPOLE	You remember it, too, miss?
CAROL	Certainly.

(MRS. FLETCHER-BREWER picks up the two pieces of cord.)

MRS. F-B	There you are!
CHARLIE	He must have done the Indian rope trick.
MRS. F-B	These are his bonds!
CHARLIE	Well, he's not in them now.
MRS. F-B	He's not in them now, but he was in them then!
CATCHPOLE	Then he must be still at large. We'd better look else-where!
CHARLIE	Yes. That's a very good place.
CATCHPOLE	Follow me!

(CATCHPOLE races off upstairs, followed by MRS. FLETCHER-BREWER and CAROL. CHARLIE goes quickly to the cupboard and opens the door.)

CHARLIE	It's all right, Harold. You can come out now.

(EDNA comes out of the cupboard. CHARLIE reacts.)

What are you doing coming out of that cupboard? That cupboard is for putting things in, not for coming out of!

EDNA	I came to and there I was.
CHARLIE	You expect me to believe that?
EDNA	It was 'im what put me in.
CHARLIE	Put you in?
EDNA	The cupboard. When I was out 'e put me in.
CHARLIE	Which he?
EDNA	He what was in there when I was out 'ere.
CHARLIE	You mean he what was in there when you were out here put you in when you were out?
EDNA	There's no other explanation.
CHARLIE	I should hope not. Well, what have you done with him?
EDNA	Who?

CHARLIE	He what was in there.
EDNA	I ain't done nothing with nobody.
CHARLIE	Oh, what a shame!
	(HAROLD comes in through the front door.)
	Harold! Where have you been?
HAROLD	It's her!
CHARLIE	Now don't you start!
HAROLD	She's after me!
CHARLIE	Quick! Behind the bar!
	(HAROLD hides behind the bar as NORAH, a little out of breath, pounds in from the front door.)
NORAH	Did he come this way?
CHARLIE	Your husband?
NORAH	Don't be daft! I'm looking for 'Arold!
CHARLIE	Oh – yes.
NORAH	Which way did he go?
CHARLIE	Well, he said he was going to bed in five minutes.
NORAH	I'll 'ave to be quick, then! (She gives CHARLIE a quick pinch on the bottom and races up the stairs, turning at the top.) Which room is he in?
CHARLIE	Oh – er – Willow.
NORAH	Willow – right! (She goes.)
EDNA	Mr. Spook's not in Willow.
CHARLIE	Never you mind. Okay, Harold. It's all clear.
HAROLD	(emerging) I'll be glad when I get out of this place.
CHARLIE	You're lucky to have women running after you.
EDNA	(suddenly) Ooh!
CHARLIE	Whatever's the matter?
EDNA	I've left the kettle boiling! (She runs off D.L.)

CHARLIE	I didn't know it was time for tea.
	(FRED comes briskly downstairs with the old suitcase that POLLY took out of the cellar. He is looking pleased with himself.)
FRED	Quick – Charlie! Over 'ere!
	(CHARLIE and HAROLD gather round as he puts the case down on a table.)
	You see before you a new man!
HAROLD	Well, I didn't much care for the old one.
FRED	Notice anything about me, 'Arold?
HAROLD	You're smiling again!
FRED	I'm smiling because I'm 'appy. And why am I 'appy?
CHARLIE	You've won the football pools.
FRED	While you two 'ave been playing 'ide and seek, I 'ave found the Crock of Gold! (He touches the suitcase reverently.)
HAROLD	Get away! That's only an old suitcase.
FRED	You can't go by outside appearances, 'Arold. It's what's inside that matters.
CHARLIE	Where did you get it from?
FRED	I caught the girl Polly sneaking it into 'er bedroom. So I waited till she went downstairs to fetch 'er father –
CHARLIE	And walked in and helped yourself!
FRED	That's it, Charlie boy!
HAROLD	But what's in it?
FRED	What do you think? The stuff we was after, of course!
	(POLLY comes on from upstairs in a high state of anger. She is in her pyjamas.)
POLLY	So there it is! What the hell are you doing with my case? You just give that back to me! (She comes down the stairs.)

FRED	Wait a bit! Wait a bit! It's not yours, y'know –
POLLY	Oh, yes, it is! You took it out of my room! You pinched it! You'd better 'and it over or I'll call the Police!'
CHARLIE	(to FRED) She wouldn't do that, would she?
FRED	No, of course not!
POLLY	Oh, yes, I would!

(She tries to grab the case from FRED but he quickly throws it to CHARLIE. She runs from one to another as they pass the case around between the three of them.)

FRED	Grab 'old of 'er, Charlie!
CHARLIE	What?
FRED	Grab 'old of 'er!
CHARLIE	Oh, all right.

(He grabs the girl and HAROLD throws the case to FRED. FRED misses it and it falls to the floor. As he picks it up, the lid falls open and the contents spill out. Inside the case are various items of ladies' underwear. They all – including POLLY – stare in astonishment. HAROLD picks up a slip and holds it up in front of himself.)

HAROLD	(puzzled) Is this the stuff we were looking for?
FRED	(glaring) Don't speak to me, Spook!
HAROLD	Oh, dear. You're not smiling any more, are you?

(FRED searches frantically through the case, flinging underwear in all directions. HAROLD is still holding the slip in front of himself, and CHARLIE has both arms securely around POLLY's waist as from upstairs come MRS. FLETCHER-BREWER, CAROL and CATCHPOLE. They stare in astonishment at the scene.)

MRS. F-B	What is the meaning of this decadent spectacle? Mr. Mullins! What are you doing with that young woman?
CHARLIE	The Military Two-Step!

(He releases POLLY as EDNA comes in from D.L. with a

teapot.)

EDNA	I've made the tea and that's that! (She slams the teapot down on the tray, and sees the suitcase.) 'Ere! What you doing with that suitcase?
CHARLIE	Have you seen it before?
EDNA	Of course I 'ave!
FRED	Where?
EDNA	In the cellar a few weeks ago.
FRED	So that's where it was 'idden!
CHARLIE	Did you look inside?
EDNA	Yes, of course I did.
FRED	(holding up a handful of clothes) And was this all you found?
EDNA	(casually) Oh, no. It was full of money then.

(A tiny pause, then there is a concerted move to EDNA from FRED, CHARLIE, HAROLD and POLLY.)

POLLY	What did you do with it?
EDNA	Ever such a lot there was.
CHARLIE	What did you do with it?
EDNA	I didn't know what to do, Mr. Catchpole being out.
FRED	(desperately) What did you do with it?
EDNA	I said to myself, "Funny place to keep money", I said –
FRED) CHARLIE) POLLY) HAROLD)	(together) What did you do with it?!
EDNA	I gave it to the Police!

(They all react. FRED sinks in despair onto a chair. CHARLIE and HAROLD turn to each other, unable to control their laughter.)

FRED	What's the matter with you two?

HAROLD   So all the time we've been 'ere –

CHARLIE   There never has been any money!

                (HAROLD and CHARLIE cling on to each other, laughing
                helplessly. FRED is furious.)

FRED   I'm glad you think it's so bloody funny!

                (From upstairs a sudden shout.)

NORAH   (off)   Help! Help! Help!

FRED   What the 'ell's that?

CHARLIE   (smiling)   I think Norah's met her match.

                (NORAH comes running down the stairs in a considerable
                state of alarm.)

NORAH   Help! Help! He's after me!

                (She runs past the astonished onlookers, heading for the
                door D.L. She is pursued down the stairs by MR.
                PARKINSON. He is smiling optimistically as he gamely
                gives chase.)

MR. P.   Here! Wait! Wait for me, then!

                The others all react, CHARLIE and HAROLD still laugh-
                ing helplessly, as MR. PARKINSON pursues NORAH
                off D.L.

                THE CURTAIN FALLS

PROPERTY PLOT

ACT ONE

Set:
    Dustpan and brush
        (off R. EDNA)
    Suitcase (off U.C. FRED)
    Hotel register (bar)
    Pen (bar)
    Suitcase) (off U.C. NORAH)
    Grip   )
    Fishing tackle) (off U.C.
    Landing net   ) Mrs. F-B)
    Tray (off L. EDNA)
        on it:
            Tea-pot
            Milk jug
            Sugar bowl (lumps)
            2 teacups
            2 saucers
            2 plates
            2 knives
            2 teaspoons
            Plate of bread-and-butter
            Jam
    Cup and saucer (off L. EDNA)

Personal:
    2 pieces of cord (HAROLD)

In Interval:
    STRIKE   Tea tray, pieces of cord.
    CHECK   NORAH's coat off L.
    SET   Newspaper (sofa)

ACT TWO

Set:
    Plate of ham salad)
    Knife and fork   ) (bar, EDNA)

Tray (off L. NORAH)
    On it:
        Coffee pot (small)
        Milk jug
        2 coffee cups
        2 saucers
        2 spoons
        Sugar bowl (lumps)
    Newspaper (sofa. Mrs F-B)
    Packet of sandwiches
        (off L. CHARLIE)
    Pot of coffee (off L. CATCHPOLE)
    Bottle of brandy (bar CATCHPOLE)
    Brandy glass (bar CATCHPOLE)
    Bottle of wine (cupboard, HAROLD)
    Revolver (off upstairs,
        CATCHPOLE)
    2 small suitcases (off U.C. POLLY)
    2 blankets)
    2 sheets   )
    Pillow   ) (off L. EDNA)
    1 pillow case)

In Interval:
    CHECK Fishing net (U.C.)
           2 pieces of cord (off L.)

ACT THREE

Set:
    Torch (U.C. NORAH)
    Hand bell (U.C. Mrs. F-B)
    Flower (in vase. CHARLIE)
    Delapidated suitcase
        (cupboard. POLLY)
        In it:
            Various items of ladies'
            underwear
    Bread-and-cheese (off L. Mr. P.)

Tray (off L. EDNA)
    On it:
        2 teacups
        2 saucers
        2 teaspoons
        Milk jug
        Sugar bowl
Tea pot (off L. EDNA)

COSTUME PLOT

NORAH
Skirt, sweater, flat shoes (Act I).
Dress, white apron, overcoat (Act II).
Nightdress, dressing-gown, slippers (Act III).

EDNA
Skirt, blouse, overall, flat shoes (Act I).
Black dress, white apron, maid's hat (Act II).
Nightdress, dressing-gown, slippers, bedcap (Act III).

FRED
Harris tweed suit, pork pie hat (Acts I & II).
Pyjamas, dressing-gown (Act III).

CATCHPOLE
Brown suit, bow tie (Act I).
White coat, black trousers, black tie, shoes (Act II).
Pyjamas, dressing-gown (Act III).

CHARLIE
Suit, bright tie.

HAROLD
Blue suit (too big).

MRS. FLETCHER-BREWER
Tweed suit, trilby hat, Wellington boots, raincoat (Act I).

Dinner dress (Act II).
Nightdress, dressing-gown, slippers (Act III).

CAROL
Skirt, sweater, raincoat, boots (Act I).
Dinner dress (Act II).
Nightdress, dressing-gown, slippers (Act III).

POLLY
Sweater, mini-skirt, high-heeled shoes, plastic mac (Act II).
Pyjamas, dressing-gown, slippers (Act III).

MR. PARKINSON
Old suit, raincoat (Act II).
Striped pyjamas, raincoat, slippers (Act III).

LIGHTING CUES

ACT ONE   None.

ACT TWO   None.

ACT THREE   Main lights ON (page 83).
               Main lights OFF (page 89).
               Landing light ON (page 90).
               Main lights ON (page 90).

EFFECTS

Revolver shot (Act III).

PRODUCTION NOTE

Farce has now become so popular in both the professional and amateur theatre, even receiving the accolade of National Theatre presentation, that the rules of performance and production which apply to this particular genre are by now pretty well known, and more and more companies excel in the art. I will not, therefore, repeat here the old list of rules and exhortations relating to farce. Let it be enough to quote the accepted definition — "Real people in unreal situations" — and to say that while pace is essential it must not be such that it leaves the characters with no time for thought, and that it is acquired by picking up cues neatly and not by the speed with which you deliver the lines.

There are ten characters in "Off the Hook!" and they all have their moments, the burden being spread fairly evenly between the actors. The trio of wrong-doers ("crooks" is perhaps too strong a word for such a bunch!) must be contrasting in type to provide the correct foils for each other. Charlie is pleasant, charming, easy-going; Harold, pathetic and put-upon, bearing the brunt of the misfortunes of the play; Fred, the strongest personality of the three, a forceful Cockney with plenty of attack. They must work really well together, and the success of their individual performances is dependent upon one another.

Major Catchpole is military in bearing and manner, but the fun of the characterisation is in the fact that his upper class overtones are hiding rather rougher roots, and we know by an occasional dropped 'h' or 'g' and the frequent over-refined vowels that there is a Cockney lurking beneath the surface. But this must be smoothly absorbed into the characterisation so that it does not hinder the flow of the performance. Catchpole is a bit of a snob, obsequious in his dealings with Mrs. Fletcher-Brewer but rather condescending with the "lower orders". His wife, Norah, makes his assumption of upper-class respectability rather difficult, she being friendly, effusive and down-to-earth with no pretences at all. She enjoys life to the full, is unaware of class barriers, and her pursuit of Harold and her familiarity with the other men must spring from her bonhomie and ebullience and will then give offence to nobody.

Edna is the complete opposite of her sister, both in build and behaviour. Where Norah is plump and jovial, she is parched and pessimistic, and her constant air of gloom makes her one of the most amusing characters in the play.

Mrs. Fletcher-Brewer is a gorgon, an archetype character of English farce since the great days of the Aldwych. Stern-faced and forthright of speech, she is a match for any but the most fearless. As Charlie says on one occasion, "I bet she scares the life out of them on the Bench". It is important that she is played by an experienced character actress, as the success of a large proportion of the play depends upon her. She must have a commanding voice and presence so that Charlie and the others have something very definite off which to play. Carol is in no way like her mother. She is very pretty, charming and patient. I have deliberately refrained from developing the relationship between her and Charlie any further, as this would have upset the balance of the play, but the relationship does exist and is an essential part of the fabric, a welcome lull between the broader moments.

Mr. Parkinson is very old and very deaf, and there is an obvious temptation to overplay him. Resist it, keep him real and you will be well rewarded. During the sequence in Act 3 when he is captured and tied up, he never gets angry. He is always unruffled, and his reaction is slight bewilderment and amusement at what he imagines is a game. His daughter, Polly, is blonde, sexy and mini-skirted. She and Carol are both extremely decorative but in completely differing styles.

I have tried not to over-burden the script with stage directions as I feel this is only frustrating to actors and directors who, naturally, want to evolve their own patterns of production. I have tried to limit myself to those that are essential to a situation or to the working of a reaction vital for a particular laugh. Apart from a revolver shot, the play has no effects and no complicated mechanical devices, so the director can concentrate his time solely on the actors and be able, therefore, to drill them into a well-organised team working with the precision of a machine. He will help the play enormously if he is careful to build up to a tremendous climax at the end of each Act.

The setting should be pleasant to look at, oak-timbered and comfortable, with plenty of Spring flowers about the place. Lighting should enhance the set as much as possible. This is helped in Act One by sunlight and a warm amber glow from the fire, and in Acts Two and Three by the more interesting appearance of the practicals which will then be on. But in helping the look of the set remember not to sacrifice light in the main acting areas. I have often felt sorry for actors struggling to play farce in the gloom! The only time we do not want to see well is in Act Three on pages 83 and 89, when the only lighting is from moonlight and the dull red glow of the dying fire.

I hope you will have a lot of fun working on your production of "Off the Hook!"   Good luck to you all.

D.B.